HOW TO PREDICT THE FUTURE
and what to do about it so you WIN!

by **P. Hughes Egon**[*]

World-renowned futurological predictologist

Author of the international blockbuster
The Art of Being Right About Everything

Managing Partner, **Hornsdog Partners**

and Eminent Professor at Cambrevard University

The world's preeminent business strategy manual on how to strategically use strategy, competitive intelligence, crowdsourcing, Twittercasting, value-added six sigma, long-tails, waterboarding, social media and nanobranding to ***MAKE MONEY THIS QUARTER*** (while scrupulously avoiding trends, forecasts, expert opinion, rigorously explored scenarios, open communication and clear decisions.)

[*]with Eric Garland, an underpaid ghost writer grad student type, author of *Future Inc: How Businesses Can Anticipate and Profit from What's Next*

This publication is designed to provide accurate and authoritative information in regard to the subject matter covered. It is sold with the understanding that neither the publisher nor the author is engaged in rendering legal, accounting, or other professional service.

Dr. P. Hughes Egon is a fictitious character who is not intended to represent any person, living or dead. If that is not abundantly clear, this book will be very confusing, but we thought it helpful to point out directly.

No futurists were harmed in the making of this publication. However, several egos were bruised. Management regrets the inconvenience.

Garland, Eric A.
How to Predict the Future...and WIN!!!!

ISBN-10: 0-9835595-0-3
ISBN-13: 9780983559504

Published by Wallingford Press, Saint Louis, Missouri, USA
An Agos Dynamics Group Company

Design: Lee Robinson, Playground Creative
Author photos: T.J. Hooker (inside back flap), Katy Corea (back cover)
Stock photos: iStockPhotography.com

The tragedy of modern leadership is the unbearable tension of quotidian management of the infinitely complex and the yoke of responsibility to future generations. No modern leader can ignore this responsibility; no citizen should fail to appreciate the weight of such an impossible travail. My friend and colleague Hughes Egon elucidates the path ahead with wit and candor. How to Predict the Future and Win is a work of superior intellect and humanity.

- **His Excellency Dr. Justin Bieber, PhD**, *former Ambassador to Germany and envoy to the United Nations Security Council, winner of the Pulitzer Prize for Literature, author of "My Life: First Step 2 Forever"*

OTHER BOOKS BY P. HUGHES EGON
(with Eric Garland usually, who was paid a small hourly wage)

To The Year 1980! (Spoon Press, Colchester UK, 1960)
How tube electronics will revolutionize radio-vision, the future of LSD, the futility of non-monkey space flights, and why the Soviet Union will likely win the Cold War due to its superior machine tools.

The Keith Moon Algorithm (Hi-Watt Press, London, 1968)
The world's foremost manual of predictology for percussionist morbidity and mortality. (Foreword by Robert Plant, KBE)

10,000 Heart Healthy Recipes with TOFU (Superiority Press, Chico, 1972)
Forecasts on what everybody will be eating in the future, told from our unique and superior California perspective.

The Testosterrific Future (Gekko Press, Darien CT, 1985)
Why growth, finance, money, and hugeness are the wave of the future, and you had better get out of the way unless you want to get steamrolled by tomorrow's trends. Bitch. (Foreword by Bret Easton Ellis)

The Art of Being Right About Everything (Halcyon Press, New York City, 1990)
The groundbreaking, earth-shattering tale of how I came to be the world's pre-eminent predictor of things due to my unbelievable track record of near omniscience.

Sex, Drugs, and Immortality! (Boomer Press, Boca Raton, 1995)
Why nanotech and biotech will converge in the next ten years such that the world will be "talkin' 'bout my generation" forever, and we don't have to get old, or die...um, not that we're going to because...uhh...science will fix all of it. So let's stop talking about this.

The Hugest Boom (Taurus Press, East Hampton, 2000)
Three words: DOW NINETY THOUSAND - our forecasts on how your retirement funds will almost certainly triple every year or so, allowing you a prosperous old age no matter what happens to the rest of the world.

Predictology for Kids! (Regnery Press, Houston, 2006)
Kids should also learn to predict things like growth, profit and hugeness so they can start their own hedge funds before leaving puberty.

OK, Except for the Rise of China, 9/11, and the Mortgage Crisis, I Really Do Predict Everything Correctly (Reiteration Press, New York City, 2009)
Because I do, you know.

CONTENTS

You Can Get The Future You Want, Baby

An introduction from **P. Carter Langston III**

Senior Strategical Thinking
Practice Director
Hornsdog Partners
Zoo York . London . Zürich . Sydney . Shanghai
The BRIC countries (whichever those are)
Wherever The Hotness is Next, Baby
Twitter: @StrategyGuyBaby

WELCOME to the future! Yeah, I know, it's already here, but it's also on the way. Isn't that mind blowing? Yeah, I think so!

Look, I'm as disappointed as you that I haven't yet been given a company jetpack or one of those George Jetson three-hour work days, but that's just as well. Since we're not yet in some utopian future, I get to fill my days making major cha-ching for our clients around the world. And that's the most important reason for there to BE a future, am I right?

I know you're excited to be in the world of strategy and senior leadership. THIS IS WHY YOU WENT TO B-SCHOOL! You're calling the shots, your opinion is king, you are finally applying what you read in *Genghis Khan in the Boardroom (and the Bedroom!)*.[1] Regardless, if you're in charge, that means *you get to decide what the future looks like*. That's pretty awesome from top to bottom.

Here's the danger, though: at some point the peons, the little people, or maybe even the Board of Directors (when they come off the golf course) may actually want you to elaborate on what this future looks like. It might be for a "strategy retreat" or a business plan or the rare occasion when the business press feigns interest in something other than the stock market. These aren't official or important activities, but looking at the future happens to us all every few years.

Remember the eight Ps: *Failing to plan is planning to fail!* You need a methodology if you're going to predict the future. You must learn from those who have gone before you into the morass of foresight. That's why you need to read the following strategic manual, **HOW TO PREDICT THE FUTURE**. You've got to make it to the other end of this process quickly, and with your career in one piece, so you can get back to the front lines, either making money for this quarter or preparing your golden parachute for takeoff and landing. Otherwise, you might find yourself stuck in some God-awful think tank considering trends and implications forever, and you can kiss expense account dinners and self-respect goodbye.

If you're not careful, here's what could happen if you don't have a careful plan when thinking about the future of your organization - you could end up - tragically - with:

A systems approach - Instead of thinking about your organization, which is the whole point, you'll be thinking about stuff you never hear about and don't care about. Sure, that stuff will impact the organization soon enough due to the interconnected nature of our globally-intertwined economies, but it's really going to confuse people in the meantime, and possibly make senior executives feel like they don't read enough. Look out!

---

[1] *In the unlikely event that you're a government executive reading this, I guess this includes you guys too.*

Well-researched trends and forecasts from a variety of expert sources - Instead of a loose collection of ego-driven, unexamined opinions about the future, you might accidentally create a database of trends and forecasts from a broad range of subject matter experts. You will then be in the most unenviable position of questioning the assumptions of those who are paying for the study. Again, we're here to succeed in the future, not to make people feel like there are things they don't sufficiently understand. Besides, agreeing on one set of trends and forecasts may make it impossible to play our typical game of cherry-picking information to support pre-formed conclusions. Danger, Will Robinson!

Thorough understanding of implications - If you start with a large collection of trends, you could easily fall into the next step: understanding threats and opportunities for the organization. If you're like me, you'd much prefer to do a quick SWOT analysis off the top of everybody's head and call it a day. That way, you can protect yourself from the eventual uncomfortable moment of either recognizing unseen threats or realizing that there's an opportunity out there you're not exploiting. We already know the current threats - today's competitors - as well as tomorrow's opportunity - endless global growth of the same economic system. Looking at the implication of every trend out there will only lead to depression and paranoia.

Scenarios - Discreet pictures of what the future could look like given a set of trends and actor decisions and wildcard events. Man, this is going to require a lot of work, not to mention constant follow up. Imagine how uncomfortable you will feel when your company doesn't look well positioned in each possible future. That's going to suggest to your superiors that their decisions won't automatically make them wildly successful - I'll be glad it's you saying that and not me! You'll miss the most important part of scenario planning - coming up with one scenario that pleases the current order.

Clear decision making - There's a key to leadership, and it's called *wiggle room*. The future, as we know, is totally random, so your strategy ought to look suitably random as well. A rigorous look at the future might suggest that only a few approaches will match up with major trends and their implications. You might not be able to get away with saying that your strategy is to "achieve world-class quality while providing the best growth and profitability in the industry."

Communication of your vision of the future - Talking about your view of the future could affect lots of people, radiating outward, helping you establish your brand in the minds of customers, partners and constituents and your own employees. They will expect you to follow through on these promises locking into a future that's full of hard work. To be avoided at all cost!

If you avoid these pitfalls, you too can end up with THE FUTURE YOU WANT. That means big money, the success of the current system, no unnecessary surprises, happy bosses, and Dow 90,000! There's much more to learn about what not to do in this tremendous volume, *HOW TO PREDICT THE FUTURE...AND WIN*!!! I hope you'll join us for the intellectual journey of a lifetime.

Your bonus next quarter may depend on it!

THIS PAGE INTENTIONALLY LEFT BLANK
SO YOU CAN REFLECT ON HOW IMPORTANT
IT IS TO THINK ABOUT THINGS
YOU DON'T NORMALLY CARE ABOUT.

How To Predict The Future In 25 Easy Steps

P. Hughes Egon, PhD, MBA FAAFP, KBE

Managing Partner -
Hornsdog Partners

AVANT-PROPOS

After decades of taking clients through the perilous process of spelunking the future, I consider myself the Sir Edmund Hillary of strategics. Studying the future is like a mix of reading things on the Internet and open heart surgery - it's serious stuff, and people can get hurt. That's why you need a methodology and a strategy to do strategy. You too could end up lost on the Mount Everest of Strategic Challenges, doing cardiothoracic surgery while struggling for oxygen - it just won't work right!

It has been a few decades since my best-selling blockbuster *The*

Art of Being Right About Everything became necessary reading for every prime minister, captain of industry, and African warlord on the planet. As you all are aware, the book brilliantly explored my experience accurately predicting the death rates of rock and roll drummers, a method which I then used to form Dead Pool Associates, which was then acquired by the CIA to predict which Soviet premier would expire next. *Yuri Andropov, we hardly knew ye!* As you all know, we positively owned the late 1970s prediction and futurism scene, involving tons of crazy nights at Studio 54, guest hosting Saturday Night Live, keynoting World Future Society conferences, trips to Betty Ford. This is still affectionately referred to as the Golden Age of Futurological Predictology.

The three decades which followed have been infinitely rewarding. Linking up as I did with celebrity accountant John Hornsdog allowed us to make Hornsdog Partners the most elite purveyor of executive strategic entertainment in the world. Whether snorkeling off Turks & Caicos with tobacco executives, creative visioneering sessions at Napa wineries with chemical company honchos or simply recording the sounds of our own voices to hear them played back, we have prided ourselves on helping the top 0.0006% of humanity envision the future for us all. We have learned so much about the future - specifically that while it's not a particularly scarce resource, it can be sold off at really great gross margin.

Now, it's time to bring that $30,000 per day wisdom to you, the swarthy, unwashed masses of middle management.

My publishers said it was time for an eleventh book, given the somewhat lukewarm response to my last tome, *OK, Except for the Rise of China and 9/11 and the Mortgage Crisis, I Really Do Predict Everything Correctly.* It occurred to me that the pearls of wisdom obtained through decades of custom consulting sessions would serve as excellent material for the world's preeminent manual on predictology. I had learned so much in my discussions with clients whose needs were as varied as all of the different creatures found in nature. These were the infinitely diverse questions plaguing our world's greatest leaders:

☞ *How can I keep growth going?*
☞ *How can I improve the bottom line?*
☞ *How can I get profits looking fatter?*
☞ Cutting costs while increasing the top line - *is it still the best strategy?*
☞ *Information technology - when can it just get rid of people entirely?*
☞ *Quality: can it be used to stimulate growth, profits, the bottom line, and robust stock prices?*
☞ The new age of ethical business: *that can be used to juice up this quarter's earnings report, can't it?*

There is only one way to achieve the insight required to answer these important questions - *futurological predictology*! And to take it one step further, you must predict the future and then master it so you WIN. It's OK, nobody expects you as a mere reader to know how to think ahead instinctively, which is why you leave it to the experts to tell you how easy it is.

Consider then, the 25 steps for predicting the future so you can WIN:
1. *Listen to major media exclusively*
2. *Put internal politics above external data*
3. *Underestimate new competition and fringe players*
4. *Plan based on a single scenario*
5. *Let fake numbers trump real insights*
6. *Focus uniquely on positive information; punish those who are negative*
7. *Ridicule, ridicule, ridicule!*
8. *Value the probability of forecasts by the charisma of the person delivering them*
9. *Compare the current moment to the 1980s*
10. *Wait for complete information before concluding, deciding and acting*
11. *Rely on technology and business, ignore culture, society, philosophy*
12. *Say you're looking out 20 years but study today instead*
13. *Take all of your sources from one country, preferably your own*
14. *Don't waste time thinking about individuals or small groups*

17

15. *Take it personally! Make sure your ego is the star of all visions of the future*
16. *Never make comparisons to history! Those jerks didn't even have computers!*
17. *Don't invite young people, poor people, artists, or any diverse opinions to the table*
18. *Start with the conclusions in mind, and push all information toward them*
19. *Keep the findings of the study secret - don't try to make the findings available throughout the organization*
20. *Assume that future generations will share your values, biases, superstitions, and desires*
21. *Confuse sexy with important*
22. *Never suggest the whole model may be changing*
23. *Communicate the future in the most abstract, jargony, ignorable language*
24. *Take it personally when your colleagues don't immediately believe your view of the future*
25. *Make sure this kind of analysis is a once every decade event*

For those of you too slow to perceive the brilliance and usefulness of these insights instantaneously, I will sherpa you safely through the remainder of this book to a future in which you arrive at the peak depth of getting the future you so richly deserve. In the remaining 256 pages required to justify a $24.95 major release, I will take you step by step so that even someone like you can predict the future, and win it at all costs.

You're welcome.

A Second Foreword By the "Ghost Writer"

Eric Garland

It's a Joke, People.

Dear reader, I am kidding. There is no Dr. Hughes Egon. He is a fictional character, a composite of all the specious strategy gurus, bloviating keynote speakers, and empty suits that talk about "the future" while actually remaining laser-focused on the next five minutes. His ideology is a distraction from actual foresight, one we can no longer afford in this world of unprecedented complexity. This book is a cathartic way to poke fun at Egon, and the very real people who think like him, so that we can create smarter organizations, ones that will thrive in the disruptions that await us. Hopefully, you will see some silly behavior that has driven you nuts, and you can have a good laugh.

But beyond its humor, this book explores a serious question that is plaguing me as a professional in the field of strategic forecasting: Why, after fifty years of increasingly advanced intellectual techniques, are we still unable to think about the future when in large groups? We have a wide variety of tools and techniques available to us to study the future, yet in the vast majority of organizations, we do not. Given the seriousness of the consequences of a lack of foresight, why don't we do more of it? Since we know that foresight leads to innovation, new products, fame and fortune - why isn't the study of the future taken seriously?

The infrastructure of the world financial system is coming apart, throwing entire countries into chaos. Industrialized nations will soon be caring for the largest generation of senior citizens in history. We stand on the precipice of peak oil production as demand climbs. Climate change is clearly taking place with its impact poorly understood. Billions lack clean water, a trend that only promises to worsen. Information technology is simultaneously setting knowledge free and creating a surveillance state.

Within these gigantic future changes there are hidden an infinite number of opportunities and threats. From these forces we face in the next century, great fortunes can be made, peace, prosperity and health can made ubiquitous- and we can face disaster. Why then is our leadership not constantly engaged in the exploration of possible futures?

I am Not Going to Tell You How to Think About the Future

It may seem odd to go in a satirical direction, to show people how not to think about the future through the twenty-five anti-techniques presented in this book. Shouldn't I be inspiring you to seize the great potential in the future? Would it not be better to give you the tools you can use immediately so that you can see over the horizon, invest early in a profitable opportunity, outwit your competitors, delight your customers, and make bags of money?

Yeah, I already tried that. So has every futurist of the last forty years or so.

The world of managerial thought is already filled to the brim with positive exhortations to think about the future that don't really work in practice. Dozens of authors will show you how you can take the long view, get there early, study megatrends, think about the extreme future, get future savvy, avoid future shock, think like a futurist, create futures, think in fast-forward, and so forth. The approach varies, the techniques might be aimed more at senior executives or laymen, but the theme is almost always the same: think about the future and take action.

I myself contributed to the canon of futurist literature with a book entitled *Future, Inc: How Businesses Can Anticipate and Profit from What's NEXT*, a manual on how to think in terms of systems, make decisions based on reliable trend data, create multiple scenarios, and create a future-focused organization. While the distillation of a distinct methodology was my own, the root material was gleaned from forty years of the modern managerial practice of foresight, specifically as applied by futurists and strategic forecasters.[2] My particular niche was to provide any person an understanding of how to think about the future, without too much technocratic jargon.

The book came out in 2007. It sold OK. It got translated into Korean and Chinese, which was cool. That said, you will perhaps notice that the world did not immediately begin producing a horde of future-loving leaders prepared to scenario-Delphi-alternate-backcast our species to a new level of evolution. In fact, you may have even noticed a bank or two on fire.

---

[2] *I ripped off the best ideas from the smarter people who came before me. This approach has a rich tradition behind it.*

Since the publication of Future, Inc., I have come to a somewhat acerbic observation about the whole enterprise of thinking about what's next: it is simply not working. The vast majority of managerial regimes remain focused on short-term crisis management, rather than a rational, long-term approach to risk management and opportunity development.

We cannot even get ourselves out of the way of the disasters that are easy to forecast. Consider the meltdown of the global financial system. Has there been a more absurdly predictable catastrophe in history? The trigger event for this disintegration started with the "sudden" collapse of the subprime mortgage market, but the roots of the disaster were obvious well in advance of 2008. The Case-Shiller Price Index, which tracks home prices in real dollars, nearly doubled in just five years, between 2001 and 2005, after a century-long period of relative stability. Mid-level bureaucrats in the United States suddenly were allowed to move into suburban tract homes the size of European castles, irrespective of any real increase in wages. Despite zero growth in real GDP, bankers were taking home bonuses bigger that most state budgets. This mad real estate bubble "growth" was fueled by financial instruments with usurious interest rates, with millions of "ARMs" timed to jack up in 2007 or so. Regulation of the financial sector had been eviscerated, especially for consolidated banks whose legal departments and lobbyist groups were often better staffed than the entire government agencies amusingly assumed to have some control over the industry. Add to this bouillabaisse of calamity the frantic selling of trillions in unregulated derivatives so complex that they would give a CPA a stroke.

The whole story took about ten years to develop, starting with the crash of tech stocks in 2001 and ending with the bailout of the entire financial industry in 2008 and 2009. All the trends required to see this scenario unfold were available to the public, for free, if anybody cared to look. There was no conspiracy. Yet the world acted shocked. After all, NOBODY COULD SEE THIS COMING.

Nobody except, somehow, my friends and I, who could not imagine any bank surviving after it approved one of our buddies for a $300,000 first mortgage when he had never held a job and was still living on student loans. Nobody could see it coming, except Nouriel Roubini. Nobody except Peter Schiff. Nobody except the hedge funders, who realized that the ratings agencies were giving AAA ratings to packets of absolute garbage, and who then shorted mortgage-backed securities, making billions.

NOBODY COULD SEE IT COMING! And then, all the same authority figures were allowed back into their pre-crash positions in the media, free to begin spouting their forecasts again, as if recent events did not completely eviscerate their reputations as prophets of the future. Right on cue, many leaders began the inevitable cycle of saying that we need to just get through this one short-term crisis before we deal with the less-important concerns of the long-term.

Is this the result of a million keynotes by futurists, of thousands of "strategic foresight groups," of innumerable executive off-site retreats? Is this the organizational culture we have created in banks, in city planning offices, in government agencies? How could we have so many organizations - financial firms, regulators, legislators and companies in related industries - so blind to the long-term future that they miss even the biggest and most pervasive catastrophes?

My colleagues will be displeased to hear it, but if futurism's goal was to change the mindset of modern bureaucracies, the meltdown of 2008 proves that it has failed. The central messages of 20th century foresight have gone largely unheeded. And, sorry to say it, the disciplines of competitive intelligence and strategic planning don't fare much better.

That's not to say that the outwardly-focused and forward-thinking insights offered up by these disciplines are wrong, but they are not taken seriously by the majority of leaders, and it is time to take responsibility for that. The notion of using intelligence about the outside world to make decisions is not working properly, and this demands serious analysis. Before we write more reports, go on any more strategy retreats, or blather on about how nanotechnology will soon cause The Singularity and eliminate all poverty, suffering and bad breath, it behooves us all to consider the root cause of a lack of foresight in our organizations.

It is not that the study of the future is somehow incoherent as a managerial discipline. In fact, it has one of the best, most consistent methodologies of any intellectual field. Understand your strategic system, collect the best trends possible, talk about the potential implications, see the world in terms of scenarios, and you will get something of value out the other side. It is just that when you see the curricula of the world's educational programs in business and public administration, rigorous foresight is rarely, if ever, included.

Find me an MBA who can graduate without being able to read a profit and loss statement, or create an 85-page Excel spreadsheet. And then find me an MBA who is fluent in the language of intelligence, trend analysis, and forecasting. The former is considered hard science, responsible management, and the latter is seen as soft and optional.[3] Never mind that honest accountants and CFOs will tell you that most quarterly earnings reports take more poetic license than Oscar Wilde and employ more dramatic exaggeration than Hunter S. Thompson after an amphetamine binge; we teach our executives to think of statistical metrics as essential and forward-thinking decision making as recreational. The world has spoken - it would rather have fictional numbers and a false sense of engineering-like control rather than a culture of open minds about the strategic future.

This might be the paragraph when the futurists and consultant types protest that they help their clients achieve a culture of foresight and that the above sentiment is too negative. In true modern, hard-number, analytical style, I would like to ask those same people what percentage of those clients would consider futures studies essential to every executive's tool box. Five percent at best?

Just from an anecdotal point of view, this author has explained his vocation to thousands of basically sophisticated people at cocktail parties, and a sizable proportion of those people treat the profession of "futurist" as slightly less legitimate sounding than "professional jellybean smuggler."[4] It is time for futurists, forecasters, strategists and leaders alike to ask why this is so much the case.

Modern Bureaucracy Sabotages Foresight

The reason why foresight never really catches on is bureaucracy. The need for stability and self-preservation in a given bureaucracy trumps transformative strategy in nearly every situation, irrespective of the seriousness or obviousness of the intelligence collected. This is not a cynical analysis, or a way to let us off the hook, go home, kick the cat, and complain about the Dilbertesque organizations we have to deal with. Recognizing the reality of bureaucracy in no way means we cannot attempt to build a

---

[3] *"Waste of time"*

[4] *Others equate the profession with the moral equivalent of pyramid marketing schemes, if that's any better.*

culture that perceives future risks and rewards. Thus, it is high time for us to look at the behavior of otherwise talented, charismatic, well-meaning, articulate, brilliant people when they form into groups.

Most people honestly want to think about the future and make better decisions. It's just that on the way to such thinking a bunch of other stuff happens. They have staff meetings, quarterly earnings due to Wall Street; the entire banking system collapses due to crazy financial instruments. New CEOs come in and fill key positions with their trusted lieutenants from other companies, and political Gordian knots ensue. They just lose hope. They change careers. No matter the commitment to foresight at the moment, when the strategy retreat is in the rear view mirror, when the inspirational keynote is done, they return to the stricture of bureaucracy and a bunch of other things unrelated to foresight arise and take precedence.

Finally, it is time to be honest with ourselves about why this is true and fix it. It is not an impossible task. The vast majority of leaders with whom I have worked either long for the freedom to think critically and create freely, or have forgotten that it was even an option. I remain optimistic in my belief that most people seek connection, creativity, and positive outcomes if they believe it is possible.

To achieve this lofty goal, we must see bureaucracy as a double-edged sword, not as the enemy. One edge of the bureaucratic sword is quite positive. When motivating thousands of people at once, established hierarchies and policies keep us from devolving into total chaos. A government agency of many thousand employees would be cripplingly ineffective if there were no policies to keep cliques and feudal-warlord-wannabes from taking its resources in one hundred directions at once. IBM, without recognized, binding best practices, would just be billions of dollars flying about in haphazard directions, nary a goal in sight. Leadership hierarchies, established policies and metrics for success are good ideas for big organizations with diverse employees and global reach.

On the negative side, a couple of characteristics of bureaucracy structurally prevent foresight from taking hold. One issue in the failure to achieve foresight pertains to organizational culture. When it comes to management, morale is more important than intellectualism. It is almost always more important to maintain stable relationships than it is to be right.

Married people reading this book must certainly recognize this reality.

Being right in some absolute sense is cold comfort when you are sleeping on the couch or ducking flying crockery. And so it is at work. Being right about the future, if it flies in the face of your organization's culture - or much worse, the existing decisions of people above you in the bureaucratic hierarchy - will do you no good when people take it as a sign of not being a team player. A strong commitment to foresight can all too often result in a stalled career or a one-way ticket to surfing Monster.com from the warm confines of a coffee shop.

The second characteristic is that the primary goal of bureaucracy is to preserve itself. Bureaucracies almost never become smaller voluntarily; bigger is better. In this twilight of the 20th century capitalist industrial system, our established institutions, both public and private, are retrenching at an incredible pace - merging, digging in, becoming ever larger. The United States is now inhabited by a very few major corporations and government agencies, representing ever larger chunks of our GDP, reducing the robustness of the system to react to unexpected events. We have ever fewer megabanks, several of which have started vast retail networks to replace small, regional banks. Pharmaceutical companies have pursued a strategy of mergers for years, leaving the world with relatively few players. Automotive companies have merged to the point of each industrial powerhouse having one or two large companies making the most important of consumer goods. And of course, all of this requires ever more centralized regulation from national and supranational governments. There is a reason that regulatory bodies are increasing in importance: should the system of a few large players receive a shock, bailouts are required to keep the rest of the system from collapsing. In the years since the financial crash, we have proven that this behavior is not a hypothetical, but, instead, standard operating procedure. This sweeping behavior, in contradiction to our putative free market principles, is due to the fact that government policy makers are indeed correct - if any part of the bureaucratic infrastructure of the global economic system comes apart, it is impossible to predict the depth and breadth of the disruption.

No doubt, there is great uncertainty when large institutions fail. The questions plague us: What if we let a couple megabanks fall apart? Would there be food riots or 10,000 community banks? What if a major economic power has its automotive industry eviscerated? Would it free up creativity and available skilled labor, or will it result in a multi-decade depression?

For now, our leaders are only willing to err on the side of keeping large institutions in tact at all cost. And in this world of a few large bureaucracies, we are all more at risk to disruption.

Foresight is No Longer Optional

In this world of entrenched, unwieldy bureaucracies, foresight seems impossible. It is tempting to throw up our hands, declare humanity a bit of a lost cause, and go on with trying to get through the next few weeks. That's what people usually do. Perhaps in past years, this type of worldly ennui and managerial nihilism was acceptable, or at least not fatal. Today, we simply do not have that luxury. The systems that keep our world running are now of a complexity that we can barely comprehend. The penalties for continuing with old mindsets in this new world will be dire given the sheer number of people currently on Earth. If we are to create a just, healthy prosperous world and avoid calamity, our organizations must become future-focused.

The strategic reality of leadership in the early 21st century does not lend itself to blindly ignoring the longer-term implications of our decisions. First, our economic and industrial systems are now superconnected throughout the globe in ways that only a tiny fraction of the population can imagine. As a result, the slightest disruption can set off chain reactions elsewhere in the system that will appear impossible to predict or mitigate.

Take for example the far reaching impact of the September 11 terrorist attacks. Within weeks of the planes hitting the Twin Towers, a cocaine epidemic was raging in Mexico as a result. The attack caused the United States to clamp its border extra tight, especially where shipping vehicles were concerned. The U.S., with its large population and relative affluence, is a major market for illegal drugs of all kinds, the end of a long supply chain that stretches south to Bolivia. Cocaine starts as coca leaves in the High Andes, wends its way to Colombia or other parts north for conversion to powder cocaine, and then onto storage and distribution further north, usually Mexico or the Caribbean. After 9/11, the product was stuck in its storage depots, unable to progress to its final destination.

What happens when any store has a product stacked up in too great a quantity? "Warehouse prices direct to the consumer! Everything must go this weekend! Our prices are IN-SANE!"[5] Average Mexicans would normally be unable to afford cocaine, but at warehouse prices, it was suddenly a whole lot better than huffing gas or chugging plain old tequila. For months and years after, the Mexican government was swamped with a wave of crime related to cocaine addiction that overwhelmed judicial and law enforcement agencies. The normal stability in the price of cocaine kept illegal drug usage patterns fairly stable, but because the world is now so tightly superconnected, a terrorist attack 4000 miles away resulted in a sudden and dramatic disruption.

Another reason the stakes are higher: there are simply more people in the world. A ballooning population means that the potential for humanitarian disaster is greater than ever. For example, the fluctuating cost of petroleum can have dramatic effects on the production and distribution of food around the world. The sudden high cost of gasoline in 2008 sent the price of grain skyrocketing around the world, resulting in food riots in Asia. One of the reasons petroleum costs were fluctuating was that the bank meltdown sent investors from potentially-intangible assets like cash into hard goods that would not devalue in the event of further collapse of the U.S. banking system. If complexity can mean bread shortages in record speed, and ultimately the potential starvation of millions or billions, we must think deeply about the implications of what we do.

What's more, the world will have even stronger shocks to the system than terrorist attacks and financial bailouts in the years to come. If you follow the beliefs of Nassim Nicholas Taleb in *The Black Swan*, we cannot even be sure what they will be. Our institutional design is not robust or resilient enough to survive this uncertainty and complexity without sophisticated leadership. This is why tomorrow's leaders have an incredibly demanding job waiting for them, one that will require a professional level of foresight.

Beware the Traps of Fake Foresight!

It is time to reclaim the original promise of futurism, though for this brief moment, let us consider how and why we likely won't look at the future.

---

[5] *For those not originally from within the broadcasting reach of the New York metropolitan area in the 1980s, this is a reference to Crazy Eddie's electronics whose prices were also IN-SANE. He went to prison for fraud based on a very clever accounting trick. So much for the unimpeachability of numbers.*

I've collected twenty-five bad behaviors that are common to a variety of organizations. Names will be changed to protect the guilty, though nobody is innocent - from cabinet ministers and CEOs down to interns, and even us futurist consultants.

To help you along, I am employing Dr. Hughes Egon to show us precisely what not to do. For the record, Dr. Egon does not represent any one futurist, economist, CEO or pundit.[6] He is more like the collective id of the legions of expensive-suit-clad faux-intellectuals in the public arena who use the word "future" to passionately describe the status quo.[7] Egon is the soul of all the fake leaders in the world who are feathering their nests while tearing apart the value created by generations of entrepreneurs and talented executives who practiced responsible management with patience, foresight, forbearance. His is, unfortunately, a fictional character based all too much upon real events.

After Dr. Egon has his say, I'm going to be compelled to add the future intelligence view, my philosophy of rational, data-driven foresight, to see if we can put these foibles on the path toward wise management. It is not enough to say that our managerial techniques are not working; we need to identify options for how to do things differently.

The rewards will be great if we can redesign management for the future. The penalties for failure will be just as great.

---

[6] *Seriously, I'm not pointing at any one person in particular, and for the record, I am guilty of a significant amount of what I'm about to mock. Names have been changed, but we're all a little guilty.*

[7] *OK, all right, I have a couple of pundits in mind who think futurism is no more than "driving toward a brighter more profitable future" and who couldn't name three strategic, global trends under pain of death.*

The Twenty Five Steps to Predict
the Future and Win

I n my decades of experience, I have distilled the wisdom of how to predict the future down to twenty-five steps. Not twenty-four, nor twenty-six, but twenty-five.[8] These are the steps most preferred by the Fortune 500, the CAC 40, the Magnificent 7, and Sum 41 in their explorations of what is coming next. They will definitely work for you if you *apply the system* and *systematize the application*.

Incidentally, I strongly warn you not to use these insights as the jumping off point for your own reflections. I think it should be quite clear after the two introductions that strategical thoughtleadership is a high-risk, high-reward business that should be best left to people who are professional prognostical intellectuals. There is a good reason why people of our unique persuasion tend to remain in school well into our thirties - and it's not our love for one-bedroom apartments and fear of committed relationships.[9] It is that serious stratelogical

---

[8] *OK, actually my publisher gave me a study that shows business books sell better when you have a non-prime number of recommendations, and that the best sales come from books with recommendations that are divisible by five. I actually have about seventeen, but work with me as I stretch things a bit.*

[9] *Maybe a little.*

analysis takes decades, sometimes centuries to formulate. Should you attempt your own analysis of situations based on your own special perspective, perhaps even using language that is open and accessible and makes sense to your colleagues, I must take pains to warn you, *loss of limbs may occur*. Foresight is all fun and games until someone puts out a spleen.

That said, feel free to begin thinking about the future using this carefully designed system. I can personally guarantee that if you create strategies for your organization using the precise techniques I describe, you will most certainly achieve the quality of foresight for which an increasing proportion of our institutions' leaders are so deservedly notorious.

Let's get started.

Tip 1

LISTEN TO MAJOR MEDIA

EXCLUSIVELY

E very important point being made is being
reported on in the major media. That's how you
can tell it's safe information. Don't go listening
for weak signals of trends in the making as
reported by some bathrobe-clad amateur's Twitter stream. If it hasn't
been on the television yet, why bother? Do you really want to go
digging around scholarly journals, following expert blogs, or more
distastefully, asking the opinion of someone not yet famous enough
to warrant a talk show gig?

A corollary to this is: if a famous pundit hasn't said it, it's not an
opinion worth having. For that matter, your final analysis of trends
should be a collection of opinions that have already been held by
people writing in major newspapers. The future is easily available in
major media. You'll pick truly useful information on a daily basis such
as, "Today's big crisis: why nobody could see it coming" or "Today's
crisis: why I have been warning people all along about this in my past
twelve books which you should pick up." Precious little ink (or pixels)
will be wasted on things like "uncertain trends about what's next."

And don't go digging into some pundit's actual professional-level work - wait for the soundbites to come out. Sure the New York Times' Paul Krugman has actually done Nobel Prize economic work. But really, who is likely to base his view of the future on Krugman's work on currency crises, location theory, and economic geography? [10] Wait for him to say simple and useful things destined for the masses such as, "Hey, it doesn't matter if the United States runs structural deficits like a bunch of coke-addicted African finance ministers. We're not Greece!"[11] Isn't it better to express unexplained faith in America's ability to run endless debts rather than fall into some rhetorical battle about liquidity traps and decoupling in the new economic geography? Go USA!

As far as all of those other sources: Blogs? Forums? Guys on Twitter with fewer followers than Ashton Kutcher? Are you kidding? What could they know that Ashton doesn't?

>>>>>>>

The future intelligence view: Authority is at a turning point.

We're at a critical point in terms of authority. The vestiges of 20th century mass media are dissolving with incredible rapidity. In its place, we are relying more and more on social media, which loses conflicts of interest at the same time that it corrodes the automatic credibility that was associated with mass broadcasting. Essentially, we're faced with a dilemma - to whom should we listen? On whose insights should we rely?

It is difficult to underestimate what a revolution this really is, and like many revolutions, a complete chaotic mess. The average individual in a

---

[10] *If you're insane you can actually look up* **"Krugman, Paul, 'Increasing returns and economic geography'** *- Journal of political economy, 1991 - UChicago Press"- or you can read his three line blog posts for the New York Times. It depends on how much time you really want to waste in this brief time in the mortal coil.*

[11] *Krugman's "Lost Decade Looming" said we should run some more deficits, baby! http://www.nytimes.com/2010/05/21/opinion/21krugman.html?dbk*

World 1 democracy[12] is inclined to define him/herself as someone who exercises free will, drawing understanding of reality from a variety of sources and choosing a descriptive narrative of what's happening without interference from some self-interested third-party, like a church or a nation state. However, the fact is that we all depend on authority figures to make any sense of the world at all, and their weakening puts us in a position where we must rethink a great deal of how we make decisions.

Why do we have all of this dependence on officially-sanctioned authority figures to determine credibility? It is only natural when you consider the unfathomable complexity of the modern world. Whereas people in past generations may have actually met most of the other humans who helped them feed, clothe and defend themselves, the supply chains of the modern economy are so bewilderingly interwoven that no one person really understands how all of their goods and services get to them.[13] Even today's polymathic geniuses are completely ignorant of an overwhelming proportion of the available knowledge used by the modern world. Past geniuses like Thomas Jefferson, Voltaire and Benjamin Franklin may have been well-known experts in law, agriculture, diplomacy, science and the trades of the day, but the cumulative knowledge of those fields was a tiny fraction of what exists over two centuries later. Most of us are lucky if we end up mastering a portion of one of those fields. In fact, careers now depend on deep mastery of a niche, not broad-ranging general knowledge. We thus need to rely on authorities in their respective fields to understand everything from cooling vegetables at groceries stores, to running a daycare, to producing cutting-edge oncology research. We are at the mercy of authorities, and to undercut the ability to believe in their expert knowledge, without a way to replace it for the purposes of our decision making, is confusing at best and dangerous at worst.

The Internet has ironically conspired to make mass media even more sensational and less useful. The ability to track clicks for each page has been

---

[12] *World 1: Wealthy nations with upper and middle classes, generally democracies. World 2: China, India, Ukraine, and other countries with burgeoning industry in which most basic needs of the population are met. World 3: Countries facing gross inequality, poverty, disease, illiteracy. World 4: Sierra Leone, Somalia, Baltimore.*

[13] *My favorite definition of complexity is, "A system so large that no one person can understand all of it without the help of others."*

driving our intellectual culture further and further into a fever swamp of celebrity nip slips[14] and American Idol heartthrob fascination. There is an old trope in the advertising business, "Fifty percent of the money spent in advertising is totally wasted - we just don't know which fifty percent." Today, perhaps unfortunately, we know exactly which advertisements hit their target markets. The Internet allows us to measure, click by click, which bit of information draws eyeballs, and which stories are forgettable and unprofitable. From a marketer standpoint, this is good news - we can now assure that our money is spent hitting the target demographic with considerably greater accuracy. From the point of view of intelligent media consumers, it is a catastrophe. We are virtually guaranteeing that the major media will feed us a diet of increasingly sensationalistic pabulum in order to slake their advertisers' thirst for more clicks. Back in the days of dead-tree newspapers and one-way broadcasts, editors had to put out a rich mix of investigative reporting, colorful entertainment news, a sprinkle of gossip, really dry science reports, a bit of fall fashion - whatever gathered a sufficiently large demographic to be able to resell to advertisers. Now that they know where their clicks come from, editors are obliged from a business standpoint to run the stories that sell clicks.

The list of stories we are now fed from major media includes, but is sadly not limited to: missing middle-class white girls, extremist political rhetoric, how some people are getting rich quick, the latest pronouncements on which foods cause/cure cancer, any story where a couple of people died in some usually mundane way, celebrity divorces, and much, much less. The editors of these digital publications can now verify that their stories about major changes to the U.S. federal budget will garner but three percent of the traffic compared to a story about JonBenét Ramsey's maybe-murderer being caught in Thailand. There is no question about which story to put on Page One.[15]

When thinking about the future, sensational infotainment - sadly omnipresent in major media - is a speedbump on the way to real insights. The future, by definition, presents itself as *weak signals* before evolving into a full-blown trend that will affect your business. If you wait for trends

---

[14] *If the definition of this term is unclear to you, plug it into Google and you will understand why such stories tend to overpower similar articles about continuing budget resolutions.*

[15] *This was a real editorial decision at a major publication. And of course, the guy wasn't even the killer. So the whole thing was a waste of time, but it made money.*

and events to be reported by the major media before acting on them, you will forever be at the mercy of those actively collecting information about what's next and acting early. This is why the future of futurism is likely to be found in the gathering of intelligence from various sources and making your own judgments about the value of the information collected. It is hard, but worth the time. Nobody will be doing this for you.

I am unable to provide an easy solution to the would-be futurist leader regarding this amazing shift we are going through. The short answer is that we must be open toward the emerging voices of expertise while remaining sophisticated, skeptical consumers of the information provided to us by the established authority figures on whom we shall surely continue to rely.

POSITIVE VALUES FOR THE FUTURE:

Openness toward all voices - It is completely understandable in this world of limited time and limitless unsorted data that we need to shortcut, as much as possible, how we make decisions without going mad. If we truly considered all ideas in the world, we would turn seventy-two before arriving at a satisfactory choice of what to have for dinner on our twenty-fourth birthday. Still, the increase in complexity and breakdown in authority means that we must not take the easy way out when looking for reliable information, settling on the data served up by the heavily concentrated mass media.

Sophistication = openness + skepticism - - It is therefore incumbent upon all decision makers to become sophisticated consumers of information. It is not good enough to take information - from anyone - at face value. In the early modern period of our economy we could perhaps be expected to listen to a small subset of relatively disinterested experts to understand what was next. Today, we must balance the viewpoints of major institutions and the educated (and rapidly growing) fringe of experts who never see major media coverage.

PUT INTERNAL POLITICS
ABOVE EXTERNAL DATA

A study of the future is most useful when used as a way to carry out routine political struggles of the organization. Judge each piece of information, not on its veracity, not on its implications, but for whether it shines a negative light on the projects currently under way.

This is why you should remain looking at 1 - 5 year market forecasts instead of the more frightening 5 - 20 year data. There are no good arguments to win in the longer view. Keep it real, and keep up the political infighting. Like Sun Tzu said, "The future is won by the most aggressive warrior who makes the other guy look like a moron."

The center piece of every study of the future should be near-term data about the future of the industry with its current dynamics and all of the same competitors securely in place. This way, nobody will feel uncomfortable with the findings, and will simultaneously be able to use the results as a cudgel in any ongoing struggles over budget and influence.

>>>>>>>

The future intelligence view: Embrace the long-term.

The greatest weakness of foresight can also be its greatest strength. The weakness is inaccuracy and a lack of applicability to the next five minutes. But turned on its head, nobody can be right or wrong, and it does not have to fly in the face of today's projects. Forecasting, despite its endemic inaccuracies, actually gives you a break from the tedium of day-to-day political struggles. Bureaucratic life is often beset by the grinding ennui of arguments over stapler budgets, the color of the TPS Report covers, or feudal warfare between clashing Vice Presidents. It is amazingly refreshing to be able to say, "Folks, let's forget about us for a moment - where is agriculture going? What about mobile devices? What will the next generation be facing?"

One of the reasons for pushing a consideration of the long view is that very few people in modern bureaucracies expect to be in exactly the same place in five to twenty years. Senior managers figure they may be retired, younger talent imagines that many other opportunities may arise in such a forgiving timeframe. Using longer-range forecasts as a basis for discussion can defuse the natural tension that arises when differing factions jockey for resources and influence.

It is not by accident that a best practice of many futurists is to start the discussion at five years out. It is not that we are too stupid to realize that, yes, a great many things will take place between now and then,[16] and surely it will be impossible to simply look at forecasts and arrive at a profitable operational plan. The whole point is that a leap of five years is the minimum amount of time into the future it takes to get people to *relax a bit*. Next year? They'll probably still be in the same job with some of the same projects going - no creative impulses are welcome in that time frame. Three years from now? Who knows what job they might be in, but it will likely be the same organization. Five years...? Now that's a period of time that few people are attached to. They might change *careers* in that time period, finally indulging their long-suppressed desires to be finger painting instructors or alpaca farmers.

---

[16] *Folks, if futurists could predict events five years away with perfect accuracy, we'd be picking stocks and hedging currency with eleven-digit sums at stake, and then sunning ourselves at our compounds in Maui. And this book would never have been written, since I would be sitting in the middle of my collection of vintage Stratocasters and D'angelico archtop guitars. When I wasn't napping.*

Forecasts five to twenty years into the future may not afford you precise details about the strategy for your next six quarters, though they certainly hold the seeds of what is next. That is not the point in this case, though. The goal of foresight is to enable people to relinquish the iron grip on their assumptions in order to perceive what is coming, in all its subtlety, complexity, and uncertainty. This unwillingness to describe radical scenarios in the short-term is natural. When you forecast major strategic shift in a short period of time, you may be describing how the colleague next to you is going to be out of a job. When you start with a larger point of view, the mind can loosen up, permit itself to think cogently about what is next without fear of reprisal or (as much) ridicule.

So take the long view and walk backward from there toward implications. It will not turn a company into a happy family, but it is more likely to offer a new perspective than the same old short-term business unit-level forecasts.

POSITIVE VALUES FOR THE FUTURE:

Open dialogue - The most important thing at stake here is the ability to have an open and honest discussion about what the future will look like. As long as people are tied into their personal ambitions and sedimented assumptions, formed over decades, a real dialogue about information will be impossible. Overall, organizations need to produce a little bit less and talk a whole lot more. Open dialogue is the only way to gather sufficient data from all parts of an organization and certainly the only way to be able to understand what to do next. Unfortunately, many institutions have a culture of seeing dialogue as tantamount to insubordination. Talking about uncertainty and risk in the marketplace is viewed as a challenge to past decisions, instead of being seen as a way to protect valuable assets and enhance creativity.

A word to leaders - given the awesome changes awaiting the world, nobody's experience prepares him or her to be right all the time. One might as well be wrong, while constantly learning. It may be quite a bit more fun. So talk about the future.

Group cohesion - Hierarchical organizations, which are often necessary, tend to leave many people feeling powerless. In all but the most innovative structures, real strategic decisions are made from a centralized group of top executives, and performance is expected from all others. Fine; once the decision is made, perhaps it is necessary to insist on discipline. But discussing the long term future is a great way to reconnect the entire organization with where they are headed, individually and collectively. It returns power to everyone involved simply to be able to discuss where the world is going and how they might fit in. It is an unequaled morale booster.

When my clients study the future, they often dispatch a multi-disciplinary team from around the company to champion the idea. Sometimes it is a strategic planning department or an EVP running the project, but more often it is a collection of engineers, product managers, finance people, marketers, even interns. I have never heard a group regret its time spent studying the future. The majority lament having to go back to their "real jobs." One transportation executive told me, "the best part of my career, hands down, was in 1977 when I spent a year looking at our future. I explored enough new ideas to keep me inspired for years." Most people do not describe the year 1977 as the best of *anything*,[17] so I say this is at least anecdotal proof that looking at the future is maybe even better than cash bonuses at making people feel connected to their jobs, their colleagues, and their own lives.

Finding common ground - In speaking with executives about the future for over a decade, I have found that the best way to get senior leaders talking openly about the future is to talk about their grandchildren. Funny, most people do not feel as sentimental about their children. After all, they spend at least a couple decades trying to instill discipline and hard work into their kids, and perhaps they expect that they should be unafraid of challenges. Also, their kids may have wrecked a few cars and taken seven years to get through university. But bring up their grandkids, and you will immediately see people think about their long-term legacies, much more concerned about leaving a mess to clean up. They may not automatically care about the long-term future of their company, but do care what happens in twenty years, when their grandchildren have grown and are navigating the world? This is what they share in common with their descendants. It is their lasting gift to the ages. And the rules have not yet been set in stone for those kids. Social stratification has not yet calcified; there are no racial or economic divisions; things are still an uncarved block, full of potential.

---

[17] *Except for me, since my wife was born that year. Here's hoping she reads this far and I get points.*

The lives these children live will be decided, in part, by strategic decisions made today by these executives. There is more possibility and more risk as well. We are all share in this uncertainty. When you point it out, it opens the door to more dialogue.

Tip 3 — UNDERESTIMATE NEW COMPETITORS AND FRINGE PLAYERS

Anybody and anything worth considering as a competitive threat or investment opportunity is already a famous name. A corollary to this is to ignore the actions of famous but unrelated companies whose recent activity seem to be pointed at your core business. For example, I know that Apple appeared to have nothing to do with the music business in the early 2000s when the iPod came out, and that Apple is now the largest retailer of music in the world, but this is an example so freakish as to be uninstructive for all other industries. It's not like they are going to get into retail or anything. Or telephones - it's not what they do!

Also, make sure you look down your nose at anybody currently with fewer financial resources than you. If they aren't profitable yet, this probably means they will never be profitable, now or in the future, nor cause you trouble on the way up. Since you're the larger competitor, there is very little chance that their products or services are superior. The only thing useful they might do is get purchased by a larger company and then compete with you in exactly the same way you go to market. So for now, relax! You are still the big dog. And bigger is always better!

>>>>>>>

The future intelligence view: You never know who or what might be disruptive.

Our world is BIG right now, and this bigness is leading to serious complications. Our world features multinational conglomerates that are larger than any other bureaucracies in history. Consider that Siemens has 461, 000 employees worldwide. That's bigger than fifty-one countries admitted to the United Nations, twenty-five percent larger than the population of Iceland. And while we as individual citizens can only live in one place at a time, these bureaucracies span the globe, affect the lives of billions, and legally never die. There is no empire or dynasty in history that gives us a guide to the future of these mega-organizations.

It would seem that our society is addicted to big. Banks too big to fail, pharmaceutical conglomerates negotiating as giant blocs with their government clients, a few automotive companies left, all-too-few media outlets providing information. This recent preference for big, the assumption that it is somehow more competitive, is strange, since we know from mercantilism and Soviet communism that giant politburos do not tend to react quickly to important changes. Regardless, many executives assume that the only competitors or disruptors to worry about are those who look and act just like them - big.

Harvard professor and strategy icon Clayton Christensen would tell us all to be very mistrustful of this assumption, that it is the small, nimble innovators who win such competitive battles. Their very livelihood depends on savaging the profitable business of bloated incumbents too slow to react to market trends. I will not rehash Christensen's massive, groundbreaking work[18] in this space, but he makes a coherent case for predicting that whoever is the quickest and most innovative will win. This may seem obvious, but he describes the process in great detail. First, innovators peel off

---

[18] *http://www.claytonchristensen.com/books.html Start with "The Innovator's Dilemma" and read them all. Then go back and read Michael Porter and compare what is different between the two theories. This might actually be worth more than an entire MBA program, in this author's opinion.*

your least profitable business, increasing your operating profit and making you feel like you got rid of your worst business and that it is not a big deal. Now the smaller competitor is financed, hungry, and ready to go after even more business, perhaps changing the market dynamic for good. The incumbent is left being gnawed at by a ravenous mob of innovators, like some poor wildebeest beset by a pack of hyenas on the Discovery Channel.

When people are talking about future competitive dynamics, there is an enormous tendency to mention only the names you have already heard and come to fear. Is Siemens, Cisco, or General Electric planning to get in your business? No question, unless you are IBM, these competitors may have enough cash and clout to simply bury you. But what about the lone startup with the technology that does not look like any other? You know, the one with the CEO who is talking in broad, general terms about meeting the needs of a changing society, and how this technology is set for the next generation. Maybe he is just bloviating, talking up his book, a pipsqueak just trying to get attention from the business press, puff up the price of his shares, get out while the getting's good. Or just maybe he is there to get a revolution going. If you are not looking, you cannot even judge.

Here is who you might run into if you have your eyes open to unusual competitive threats: *Nokia*. Remember, before Nokia was a mobile telephony giant, it was some random Finnish logging supply company that happened to conglomerate into a bunch of different markets. Among their offerings of rubber boots and electrical cable insulation was the strange business of expensive mobile phones - perfect for keeping in touch while logging some far off forest north of Jyväskylä. It was only when their biggest customer - their charming neighbor, the USSR - was going out of business in the 1980s that they decided to make a radical dash to compete in the post-Cold War economy. They bet the farm on cell phones and won big. But what was even more interesting was going on back at Motorola, the leading provider of cell phones: *nothing*. Their competitive intelligence department has admitted that it did not really occur to them that some random Nordic boot manufacturer could seriously be sneaking up on them. They also mention that if they had seen Nokia on the horizon, they definitely would have taken steps to compete against them with vigor much earlier.

The only value in futures is the ability to understand and shape events before they are too big to manage. This runs counter to the psychological tendency of large successful companies and powerful nations to want to deal only with "competitors" of similar size. A cartoon ran around Washington in the years following the disintegration of the Soviet Union in the early 1990s that said:

WANTED - NEW GEOPOLITICAL ADVERSARY:

Major world superpower nation-state seeks similar for
decade-spanning low-intensity conflict.
Ideal candidate will have dominion over significant landmass,
naval capacity, modern air force, satellite states as proxies.
Must have significant R&D program requiring lavish arms spending.
Space program a plus!
Please send pictures of air force.

The joke among (all too few) savvy analysts was that the United States was focusing its strategy on the rise of potential competitors in the form of large, empire-like nation states, while in reality the shape of geopolitical power was changing rapidly to favor small, connected non-state actors who might be able to asymmetrically destabilize the global balance of power without the necessity of a traditional hierarchical structure and armies visible from space.

In fact, back in early 2001, a futurist colleague of mine at the Pentagon was trying to brief as many people as possible about this new shift toward non-state actors, like ideological groups and organized crime syndicates, and away from "the rise of a potential strategic competitor in the Asian theater by 2020."[19]

He only really got traction for this theory starting September 12, 2001.

POSITIVE VALUES FOR THE FUTURE:

Appreciation of the weak signal - The speed of the world, both geopolitical and economic, means that surprises will emerge with ever greater rapidity. This requires an appreciation for the small, the new, the mysterious, the

---

[19] *Hint: Not Laos.*

humble. In practice, managers will need to develop a curiosity about that which does not fit the current model. In no way am I the first to suggest this intellectual development, but I may be the first to say it is harder than it looks. People talk a blue streak about "early warning" but in practice it requires very intensive effort. There needs to be a collective change within organizations to provide intelligence on things that are not yet front page news and to accurately assess their true implications. Better than that, there needs to be a system in place to track these potential disruptors over the course of months and years. Ideally this is supposed to be a "strategic intelligence" department of some sort. I can count on one hand the number of organizations that actually have one. Clearly, there is work to be done.

.

Tip 4

There's only one future, and we just don't know what it is yet. This isn't a question of whether we can change the future by taking action, or heaven forbid, by raising consciousness. After all, what would we do with our current investments?

The point of a foresight project is to tell people how it's going to be. An important facet of the single scenario is that by definition it had better be an acceptable future for the organization sponsoring the study. If you think that telling people they are on the wrong path is the way to a career in futurological predictivism, you'll go the way of phrenology and balanced budgets.

Single scenarios are powerful, focused pieces of writing, attracting minds to their clarity like moths to a nuclear furnace.

- "We will be world-renowned for our excellence, which will make us number one in the world."
- "Our current investments will earn us bajillions, due to superior increases in efficiency."
- "Our brand will become so potent that by 2025, people will

49

actually worship our logo in flamboyant religious ceremonies"

Good futures work is about knowing what the future will be, and of course, being number one at all costs.

>>>>>>>

The future intelligence view: Nothing is more powerful than flexibility and resilience.

A huge pitfall in futures work is the tendency to look at The Future, a single scenario that tells you How Things Are Going to Be. As you should know, there is not one future, but a whole range of possibilities which depends on complex forces, actor decisions, and the cruel, humorous vagaries of fate.

Let's say it's 1973 and you are going to look at The Future of Nuclear Power. Well, we know that per kilowatt hour, nuclear electrical plants are less expensive and less polluting than coal-fired plants. You might be tempted, uniquely, on that data to forecast the speed of how fast various North American, European, and Asian nations could build such infrastructure. You might then make some assumptions about the spot prices of uranium and maybe some forecasts around future electrical prices and what that means.

Of course you are ignoring the potential of disasters like Three Mile Island and, much worse, Chernobyl. If you refuse to take into account the potential for negative events, then you will be focused on a single, preferred status quo scenario, one that will be wildly inaccurate. Consider that the United States has not ordered a single new nuclear plant since Three Mile Island, and now 80% of the electricity in the Midwest is produced with straight coal. If your scenario read, "A Safe Nuclear Future for Green Power," take three steps back. It might have happened that way, but it could have happened multiple other ways, too.

The whole point of describing multiple futures is that we need to pre-condition our brains and our strategic plans to be supple in the face of inevitable uncertainty. A crippling failure of management is the creation of dogmas that refuse to accept potential futures other than those envisioned in the current plan. As Dr. Egon has helpfully illustrated, the most common

Future Scenario is that "by [insert date] we will be number one in the industry doing exactly what we're doing now."

One of the most popular pieces of tripe in the managerial lexicon is "expect the unexpected." Of course, you should also be "thinking outside of the box." If you have extra time, you might be ready for someone to "move your cheese."

If we are going to grill up any timeless sacred hamburgers of managerial nonsense, these need to go first. Let's get serious. Inside a bureaucracy, you are told in ways big and small to *think in the box and only in the box,* unless you are perhaps a research fellow in the R&D lab or the CEO. If you are in the lab, nobody really cares what you're up to, and if you are CEO, nobody can fire you (except for Wall Street). If you run the company, or better yet, founded the company, then yes, thinking differently can get you branded a maverick, a genius, an innovator. Otherwise, you are a rebel, not a team player, someone who ought to flourish elsewhere, someone who "never quite fit in with our culture."

Why? Because thinking outside of the box means to see different customers for existing products - even if no market research reports confirm your analysis with "hard" numbers. It means to see potential threats in companies that are not yet in your market space, even if your colleagues will simply think that your psych meds need adjustment to attenuate your apparent paranoid delusions.

Expect the unexpected? How about instead, senior management tells you what to expect, and that had better be the subject of your next presentation. If you decide - even in your role as strategic planner or competitive intelligence analyst - that you are going to start expecting things to happen *other than* increases in quality, customer satisfaction, and sales volume, things such as disruptive technologies and potential economic shifts - well then, you might not be seen as all that effective in the role entrusted to you.

As far as moving dairy products go, that particular fable is more useful to explain upcoming layoffs and budget cuts more than a way to inspire creative analysis of a shifting marketplace. Enough said.

The good news is that conventional management talks the talk of flexibility and resilience. Now, it needs to walk the walk.

POSITIVE VALUES FOR THE FUTURE:

Openness to change - One of the self-preserving mechanisms of the bureaucracy is the way it engenders an inability to imagine things any way other than how things are, except bigger. The fact is, faced with transformative change, it is ever-less likely that bureaucracies can maintain the same shape and respond to emerging futures. This may be a threat to the obsolete 20th century industrial paradigm of hoping to ride the same job out until retirement and/or death. Well, one of the greatest reasons that way of thinking is no longer possible is that we are not dying of black lung at 56 after a lifetime in the coal mines. We are not stuck on the carburetor seal station at the car factory from puberty until death. Things are going to be evolving more quickly and more radically than we have seen in ages. Organizations will need to respond. This will mean imagining various scenarios that may or may not benefit the current bureaucratic structure. Then again, that is the point of the whole exercise.

Tip 5

Hornsdog Partners' most recent review of top executives shows that in 89% of forecasts that provided value to organizations, nearly 96.87% involved statistical analysis of some sort. I think you'll agree that numbers are important, no matter where you get them from.

If you'd like to join the ranks of the 87.6% of middle managers who don't have their opinion taken seriously, by all means ignore these findings. Please, don't ask the source of these numbers; to have them is divine enough. Even if the statistics are estimates that came straight from the hindquarters of a 24 year-old business school intern who was hungover when he dreamed them up, it sure is better than anything those non-quant-jocks can come up with. We are joining the ranks of physicists and physicians, people who have actual peer-review and clinical trial boards to examine their evidence. While the methodology shares no more in common than astrology does with astronomy, it smells like rigor and that counts for enough.

Let us imagine that one of your colleagues comes forth with the analysis that a large tech firm is buying one of your rivals, the low-cost option in your industry. You are firmly entrenched in the enterprise market for IT, and their product will now be available at consumer electronics stores around the world. The interpretation you should most likely choose is:

a) **The market dynamic is changing.** Clearly competition is moving downmarket. This may split the market and begin to destroy the lower-end of the value chain in the classic style of Christensen's example of the steel conglomerates slowly destroyed by profitable, innovative mini-mills. We should plan to go ultra-premium with our brand proposition or create low-cost products and global distribution at the lower end of the value chain.

b) **We make more money than they do and their products suck.** Our business runs at 60% margin. They run at 50% margin. Our topline sales are up 13% YOY and while their sales are supposedly up 28%, their profitability is still 10% percent less that ours meaning that their products are 10% less good. In short, they suck and we rock.[20]

The correct answer, obviously, is B. There are numbers in analysis B, and from numbers, we can make decisions.

>>>>>>>

The future intelligence view: Qualitative analysis is not optional

Metrics are useful, there is no doubt about it. Without statistical analysis, all of science and most of business would be impossible. It reduces waste, provides insight about how successful a policy *actually* is versus how successful we *think* it is. It keeps your doctor from giving you drugs that are actually increasing

---

[20] *Lord help me, these are near-verbatim quotes from a case study I can't bear to reveal. I like to leave people some dignity just because they are human.*

your risk of keeling over from a heart attack. It keeps our planes from falling out of the sky.

This assumes that we are asking the right questions with the numbers and that the numbers are accurate.

Our business culture needs to re-examine its relationship to numbers, to question our mass fetish for fake quantification. Remember, the vast majority of business news is about some set of numbers devised by somebody in a university or think tank. We look at stock prices while rarely discussing how they might actually reflect relative prosperity. We check new housing starts as if they are the *de facto* harbinger of a healthy economy to come, EVEN AFTER A HOUSING BUBBLE which served as the container for false prosperity. We print vast quantities of new currency to buy "troubled"[21] assets from banks, then we fail to ask how this will shift all the other numbers being tracked. We sputter excitely about GroupFaceTweet's "valuation" of $50 billion[22] without asking how this might re-write the rules for evaluating all the other companies out there. We use numbers for every situation in which we wish to convey to others that we understand the situation and are in all fact in control of everything.

We make sure young analysts can read a balance sheet, but rarely do we continue to ask - OK, *so what does this mean?* Sure, your head is stuck in column after column of numbers - what do these numbers represent in reality? What dynamics are being described by these data points? The use of metrics is great, but the *fetish* for metrics is fundamentally at odds with the study of the future, a discipline that will undoubtedly require us to step away from the false comfort offered by math to do actual analysis.

What do I mean by fetish? I will never forget the Gaussian copula formula, worshipped by Wall Street as a recipe for balancing a quadrillion dollars in mortgage-based derivatives such that you could be sure of the stability of the assets contained within portfolios that were then nano-sliced and sold to investors all over the world.

$$\phi_2(\phi^{-1}(F_A(1)), \phi^{-1}(F_B(1)), \gamma)$$

---

[21] "*crap*"

[22] *At the time of this writing. By the time you read it, I'm sure that FaceTwit will likely be valued at $1,300 quintillion after its new infusion of venture cash from Porknose Partners.*

This monstrosity above, with a lovely jumble of multi-variant letters and numbers, apparently convinced banks and regulators that, sure, financial products based on the cash flow from illegal aliens buying $430,000 town homes in far flung exurbs of Colorado using ARMs that will hit 13% in a year two, ought to receive a AAA rating since...uh...well... THESE NUMBERS TELL US THAT THE RISK POOL IS FINE. There are numbers. Formulas. Math PhDs. We're good.

The fake-numbered quantitative analysis tells us this: sure, pool thousands of these mortgages and sell them time-after-time-after-time as structured investment vehicles until Ben Bernanke buys the lot of them in a couple of years and we all have a hearty gut laugh. But a qualitative analysis of giving 25 year olds $500,000 for their starter homes on the dodgiest of mortgage terms is sure to arrive at some judgment *under* AAA status - maybe the vaunted "totally Ponzilicious" rating.

There is actually a reason we side with numbers even at the expense of common sense. Math is often used in bureaucracies to relieve the tension caused by having no reliable way to judge differences in opinion of managers at headquarters. After all, if we are just trading qualitative analysis, there is a threat that we will all end up simply disagreeing with no way to break the tie. What makes your opinion better than mine if it is just an exchange of rhetoric, of logic. If someone can produce a *pie chart*, though, we can look at the graph and all nod, yes, that first graph is a lot sharper curve upward, those numbers sure do go up. Up is good. We won't be fired for making a decision if we had graphs showing the numbers going up. The group harmony can then return to equilibrium.

The attempt to study phenomena through observation and rigorous analysis is the most important single principle to emerge from the Enlightenment, when men of learning found themselves at risk of burning, hanging, or worse when they dared to counter the prevailing regime's opinions. The only way civilization has moved forward from its witch-burning, heretic-torturing past of ignominy has been the reliance on the scientific method. Numbers play a big part of that, no doubt. The problem occurs when we supplant numbers for common sense and basic analysis, when we confuse writing about management with writing about physics or biology. For leaders, common sense must dovetail with available quantitative data, not be dominated by it.

Whether it is an over-reliance on popular financial indicators to understand the future needs of our customers, or managers requiring their sales people to fill out 28 sheets a day to track coffee consumed and number of syllables uttered to customers, it is time to put quantitative data in its place and return qualitative analysis to its proper role.

POSITIVE VALUES FOR THE FUTURE:

Philosophy - The French used to have this concept called a "salon" where no hair was styled, but where the merits of various ideas were discussed in great depth. Throughout the Western world, rhetoric was taught as a vital part of every education, up until recently when it was relegated to an odd sounding college activity known as the "forensics team." Before profound discussion was reserved for Davos and TED conferences, people were expected to explore the deeper meaning of the day's issues amongst themselves, spontaneously, even. Now, that kind of debate is seen as hyper-elite or superfluous. Our internal managerial debates have become dueling data-sets, battering rams of soundbites spiked with "hard numbers" to make them extra dangerous. Meaning is a luxury. In a time of fundamental change, in-depth discussion is now hardcore, serious business. It is at the very least as serious as statistical analysis.

Tip 6 FOCUS UNIQUELY ON POSITIVE INFORMATION; PUNISH THOSE WHO ARE NEGATIVE

Every manager knows that you will never get to the future if you aren't motivated enough to wake up tomorrow. This is why when looking at the future, it is important to squash all information that contradicts the current strategic direction or implies that the external situation may worsen. When employees don't believe that you're leading them to a bright future, they may go into major depression with psychotic features and burn the building down.

For these reasons, you should reward every member of your team that comes to you with good news about what's next. Consider free gift certificates for massages, comp time off, or straight-up pats on the head for analysts who report wonderful data such as the inevitability of economic recovery following massive banking failures or the inevitability of the entire market growing 14% per annum despite stagnant wages and and rising energy costs.

And in this spirit, those who suggest that numbers are going to head in some direction other than the stratosphere should be roundly denounced for insufficient enthusiasm. The HR department should suggest a tar-and-feathers approach that is not specifically proscribed by the Geneva Conventions, or can also recommend 48 hours locked in the Motivational Speech Sensory Deprivation Tank until a taste for cheery data is finally developed.

>>>>>>>

The future intelligence point of view: Don't shoot the messenger

If you're Finnish , Estonian, or Taiwanese you may not need to pay attention to this concept. There are cultures in this world in which pessimism is a key component of management.

There is something about being invaded on a semi-regular basis that makes a people open to both risks *and* opportunity. Take the Finns, a people who already live in the coldest, darkest corner of Europe, who also happen to be wedged between the Swedish and Russian empires. As if being blanketed in darkness twenty-two hours a day and surviving on nothing more than reindeer meat and melted snow was not tough enough, you also have the pleasure of being regularly raided and invaded by cruel Slavs from the east or maniacal imperial Swedes from the West. According to one executive from Tallinn, "Estonians tend to walk with their eyes cast downward to avoid eye-contact with whoever might be invading this month." As per a Taiwanese colleague: "You get accustomed to negative scenarios when you realize that on any given morning, China could roll over in its sleep and crush you." So when, centuries later, you are running global businesses, this explains why you do not punish the person who warns management of potential pitfalls. They might even get to go right to the head office.

Not in America, though, that's for sure. In the words of Adlai Stevenson:

> *"You will find that the truth is often unpopular and the contest between agreeable fancy and disagreeable fact is unequal. For, in the vernacular, we Americans are suckers for good news."*

Being American myself,[23] it is not possible for me to step back far enough

---

[23] *Actually, to be precise I am a seventh-generation native Vermonter, a sub-species of New Englander so dour and taciturn we make the puritans from Boston look like Brazilians at Carnaval. We distrust optimism and love bad news, since every year we expect Mother Nature to finally make good on her attempt to kill us by sub-50-below winter temperatures.*

culturally to understand why this is true of so many of my countrymen. Perhaps it is the centuries of high-velocity opportunity available here, combined with a need for group cohesiveness among the unprecedented diversity of ethnic groups, that makes us prefer those with a uniquely positive disposition. Throughout American culture, there simply has not been time for reflection or dissent. And while this approach may have worked when the plains and mountains of the West lay stretched out before Eastern industrialists, when the teeming, talented, hardworking masses huddled on Ellis Island hungry for opportunity, when World War II temporarily removed any major strategic competitor in matters industrial or military - it does not, perhaps, do justice to America's current strategic position. It is now time for everybody - Americans included - to begin treating positive scenarios and negative scenarios with equal weight.

The disproportionate desire for positive trend data and rosy outcomes unfortunately turns quite toxic when mixed with the logic of bureaucracy. Often, people who report negative possibilities in the external world - competition increasing, business model breaking down, oil running out - are confused with people who are challenging the decisions of today's senior management. The confusion goes like this:

"If you're telling me that this decision won't result in success forever, you're saying I'm stupid for having made the decision in the first place. Hence, you think I'm stupid, and that means your chances of getting a promotion are smaller than those of trying to pole vault over the Pentagon using a set of old chopsticks."

Here is the major logical fallacy underlying this - that *changing your mind is a sign of having been wrong to begin with.* This would only actually be true from a philosophical perspective if the world was slow to change. If you held incorrect beliefs for decades while nothing was changing, yes, an argument could be made that you are thick in the head. Consider that the profession of lawyer and doctor have been around for thousands of years, and futurists only have 50 years under their belts. A futurist in 1300 would have been pretty bored, waiting for 100 years between major technological advances. You might hear, "Sire, in 60 or 70 years, this gunpowder thing could be a big deal." Change was at a relatively glacial pace, so if you did not understand what was going on and what was next, the problem was yours.

However, in today's world when new technologies are vaporizing business models, when markets meltdown in an afternoon, when demographic shocks are rocking the system which have no analogue in history, the person who says that he/she knows everything about what is next is either operating a palm reading shop on the boardwalk, or deluding themselves. I hope that this reality can be spun into something positive - *you don't have to be right all the time because it is impossible.* All you can do - from heads of state down to shopkeepers - is your best. You look out the best you can, and hope to make a wise decision from the data available.

Also, and this is key, *it is not your fault.* Recognizing that the world is changing and presenting new things both positive and negative does not mean that somehow you were running your peanut butter company the wrong way. Things are the way they are. This is, ideally, the fundamental value of intelligence, to gather data and describe the world with minimal bias. This is not a guarantee of future success, but then again, nothing is.

This approach goes against the subconscious assumption that executives are supposed to maintain control of situations. In this world of change, perhaps illusions of control are overrated.

POSITIVE VALUES FOR THE FUTURE:

Objective analysis - The only way to look accurately at what's coming next is to take yourself out of the equation. Weigh all data, positive and negative, without judgment as to the outcome. This kind of objectivity does not mean giving up - lots of great successes have been born of tough times and impossible challenges. This is not easy, but it is important.

Good faith - I never cease to be surprised by the assumptions underlying the "shoot the messenger" approach to dealing with people in the field of intelligence who are attempting to provide analysis of a situation. The assumption is that if somebody is professionally tasked with analyzing threats and opportunities and they return negative information, somehow they are questioning the rationale behind the decision to begin with, essentially calling some executive an idiot. The only way to get around this is to have basic good faith that analysts are simply attempting to read the situation, and you can take or leave what they say. The more we punish people, the worse our organizational intelligence will become.

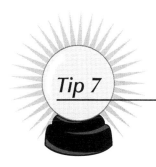

Tip 7 RIDICULE, RIDICULE, RIDICULE!

Make sure you cause junior members of your staff to feel bad about considering the long-term future implications of their work. As the average tenure at a company approaches the length of a YouTube video, the rank-and-file should ultimately become less concerned with the long-term future of whichever entity happens to be appearing in the upper left-hand corner of their paycheck this month. Future predictology should be left to senior management, consultants, boards of directors, and luxury beach resorts.

The best way to reinforce the necessary distinction between long and short-term is the useful tool of **ridicule**. While this technique was perfected by French courtiers five hundred years ago, it is truly timeless and global in its scope. And so many uses!

☞ Your entire intelligence department sees major competitors forming on the horizon from pipsqueak technology companies who fund their operations not through the flawless and meritocratic Wall Street capital system, but through group donations on PayPal. Since tiny, unprofessional companies with different approaches never really cause trouble for incumbents, this analysis is likely insane.[24]

- **Behavior modifier:** Consider offering antipsychotic drugs such as Zyprexa and Risperdal in the break room to underline how ridiculous they look by making such forecasts. Place it next to the hazelnut and French vanilla creamer with brochures to assure proper dosing. After all, these people are suffering from delusional voices telling them of unseen threats, and clearly have overactive dopamine levels in the brain.

☞ One of your rivals has come out with a new, unexpected product that meets customer requirements in a way that implies a new business model on the horizon. A product manager expresses concern that perhaps their mid-range planning sessions next month could need to take these potential new models into account, rather that plow ahead with old strategic plans.

- **Behavior modifier:** Force all of his/her colleagues to speak to this person in hushed, soothing tones reserved for anxious kindergartners, since this mentally-deficient product manager evidently imagines threats under beds and in closets and needs to be consoled like a child who is imagining things. New business model on the way? Don't worry your pretty head about it, Billy.

☞ While the TV news is blaring statistical evidence of an economic recovery that will no doubt help us reach Dow 90,000, one of the risk managers in the CFO's office keeps talking about following indicators that are a bit less biased. His concern is that many of the metrics we use to guide our understanding of the economy are insufficient to act as predictors of future business performance, since they are politicized, massaged, and scrutinized by capital markets to a degree that reduces their relative ability to describe the actual behavior of the marketplace. Obviously, this intellectual derelict has lost his mind and is demanding that you measure your financial performance in hexadecimal code and write the annual report in Klingon. Gross

---

[24] *See Clayton Christensen's new book, "Don't worry, I'm sure your position as a strategic incumbent is super safe!" now in paperback.*

domestic product, the Dow, and housing starts are sacrosanct measurements handed down to humanity by the gods and must never be questioned.

- **Behavior modifier**: Fill this risk manager's office with furniture made out of Nerf. Place plastic plugs in the outlets so he does not electrocute himself. Paint Elmo on the walls. Make sure he knows that he looks mentally unstable and that his colleagues think he could be a danger to himself.

As we know, the future is important, but it is critical that people only think about it when it is handed to them in the form of a final set of strategic plans. To help them recognize which activities are most important for them, gentle ridicule can be a wonderful guiding force.

>>>>>>>

The future intelligence view: Humility is painful, arrogance is fatal.

A troubling yet common behavior is to see all issues of the long-term as patently ridiculous. Because executives and capital markets are often myopically fixed on quarterly reports, all activities not involved with achieving that month's numbers can be seen as cost centers, detracting from the real work. Ergo, any person with career aspirations who intentionally focuses on subjects *other* than "real work" is clearly insane.

The ridicule comes in a variety of forms, subtle and overt. Raised eyebrows, condescending responses, stifled guffaws and rolled eyes are the more subtle forms. These behaviors intensify on up to the *coup de grâce* of the world of ridicule, ringing out with a hearty admonition toward people wasting their time on future trends, preferably at a meeting with lots of people in attendance.

That is not a hypothetical behavior - it was actually intoned at a meeting I myself facilitated for a client, one that was specifically reserved for future scenario thinking. During the actual proceedings, a senior vice president finally reached his limit of prognostication - an hour, by the way - and decided on the spot that the whole matter was absurd. Oh, he didn't question the validity of the data or fire back about our wrong-headed implications - the guy just thought futures was a stupid concept. He finally grumbled out, *"You know, in my 35 years experience I have learned that there will always be people who worry about the sky falling, and there will be those who worry about getting things done. And you people had better be worrying about getting your numbers up, and soon."*

The rest of the people in the room lowered their eyes, chastened for daring to think about the future during a retreat about the future. The remaining hours of the day were then spent listlessly discussing how to get more product out to more channels while cutting cost, ideally before the end of the quarter.

Ridicule is poisonous. It not only tells people to focus on something else right now - occasionally necessary, I am sure - but it assaults people's character, telling them they are frivolous and stupid in their instinctual sense of what is important. And it is only natural for many people to have nagging doubts about all the new data crossing their minds in an era of constant change. In our subconscious, we know that the world is changing in ways big and small, and we wonder what it will mean. If we are to care about the much-vaunted "weak signals" then we absolutely need the humility to pay attention to such matters. If it is seen as ridiculous on its face, if our cultures do not appreciate this as a matter of course, we risk reckless decisions that will be cemented through groupthink.

POSITIVE VALUES FOR THE FUTURE:

Respect - Sometimes ideas come across as crazy, opportunities as pipe dreams, potential threats as cranky paranoia. I myself grit my teeth when I hear about the Singularity enabling us to live forever by uploading our personalities into our iPods through ultra-advanced nanobiotech - *but you know, maybe those guys are onto something.* We must learn to listen with respect and curiosity to derive the best insights for leadership. Sometimes it means suffering fools gladly, sometimes it means humbly listening to unlikely sources and receiving vital intelligence early.

Tip 8

Value The Probability Of Forecasts By The Charisma Of The Person Delivering Them

trategic ideas should be judged based on their like-ability, not their use-ability. It is essential to make sure that the message is deliverable by someone who fits a classical definition of an authority figure. Aim for somebody who is either a best-selling author or a millionaire former tech entrepreneur. Some other guides for your spokesmodels for the future:

- White males with straight teeth and deep speaking voices are exceptional examples- though don't forget pretty white women!
- Journalists who don't wear ties and who write for arts/business magazines: also acceptable.
- Former CEOs who, against all odds, achieved stupendous growth during the largest economic expansion in history

After all, what use will your analysis be if nobody ever hears it? And who wants to listen to somebody who isn't worth listening to? So straighten your posture, bleach those teeth, and buy yourself some expensive-yet-casual-looking clothing that says you would be equally at home at top brainiac conferences, Hollywood sets, or Manhattan dinner parties. Otherwise…who are you and why are you talking?

>>>>>>>

The future intelligence view: Dispassionate analysis should be at the heart of your plans.

The challenge to authority figures, as outlined in the first "tip" of this book, presents problems that reverberate throughout our bureaucracies. To recap, there is a reason we have a positive connotation to the word "authoritative." Normally, when somebody does significant research into a subject or becomes a master craftsman, he attains a level of automatic respect for his opinions. On the subject of luthiery, the opinion of some kid working at Guitar Center has significantly less automatic credibility than John Suhr, president of Suhr Guitars and a former craftsman of boutique instruments at the Fender Custom Shop and for Pensa-Suhr.[25] Talking chimpanzees? Yes, that Jane Goodall seems to have paid her dues. Talking about the future of HIV treatment? You could read a whole bunch of webpages from a variety of authors, some clinical, some popular science and some just plain old rumor. Then again, Dr. Anthony Fauci, one of the discoverers of HIV is still in practice at the U.S. National Institute of Allergy and Infectious Diseases - you can probably give him a call. With good reason, their opinions hold weight in measure to their accomplishments in their respective fields.

That said, elite opinion has a negative side. People who have risen to prominence in a given system have done so because their beliefs and practices dovetailed perfectly with the requirements of the day. They are certainly authoritative about their world *as it is*. What about the world as it could be, might be? The mindset that masters current reality may be hesitant when it comes to saying, "You know, everything I learned in my life actually might be pretty useless in the future." To think otherwise is to possess a maturity rare in the vast majority of people. It is far more often that you encounter someone buttressing an outdated view of reality with

---

[25] *I have his boutique versions of a 1954 Stratocaster and 1970 Jazz Bass, and they are beyond awesome. Also, there's no publisher for this thing, it's my book, and I'll talk about guitars if I want to, just like in the rest of my waking life.*

the phrase, "Why, I've been in this industry for [insert number higher than twenty] years, and it's impossible that [x] will ever come to pass."

Also, mastery and authority in the modern world requires an incredible focus on one subject. The increasing achievements in science and the continuing complexity of globalized economies have all but assured that any expert cannot spend too much time on "cross-disciplinary" activities. Given that the future is about interconnection, people laser-focused on one subject are somewhat less likely to free themselves up to proffer visions of the future based on a variety of forces. Thus, they cannot be the only source of your information.

From a practical perspective, if you want to watch a foresight project grind to a halt, make it about opinions and ego. The whole point of methodology is to draw people out of their assumptions and their immediate needs to let their brains work on untangling the complexity of the future. If the landscape is covered with the large egos of highly successful, charismatic leaders, it will be markedly more difficult to get people to admit areas of knowledge where their knowledge is incomplete. Look, the future is the one thing we are all pretty ignorant about by nature, and a room full of people unwilling to admit doubt is not necessarily the best recipe for daring insight. This is not a proscription against working with smart successful people, but it is a reminder that if that is your working group, you need to take the facilitation aspect of the project very seriously. Fairly strict ground rules will need to be established to allow all the interesting, creative things to come out of such a strong dynamic.

After years of presenting intelligence reports, I have learned to greatly mistrust whatever currency might come from being tall/cute/Belgian/authoritative or whichever charisma crutch supports the credibility of your opinions. The reason being that if your findings are at all negative, charisma usually counts for nothing. Thus, do your homework. If people don't like what you have to say on its face, your clients or colleagues who requested the analysis will likely search for the most minuscule inconsistency in order to continue denying whatever uncomfortable fact you are bringing to the fore.

I remember one study on future competitive dynamics of computer retailing that was a compelling, impeccably-researched[26] project that

---

[26] *Y'know, if I do say so myself.*

showed that our client was, unfortunately, heading in the wrong direction in terms of a couple of techniques to motivate sales staff when compared to his competitors. Moreover, the study showed that this problem could be easily fixed. Having staked his reputation on our study confirming his biases instead of challenging them, he was not happy about the findings. In a fit of pique, he scoured the entire report for typographical errors and decided that our misspelling of the name of industry expert Dr. Myron Grabowizski[27] as reason enough to doubt the rest of our "shoddy" report and its "insane" conclusions. I'm not convinced a well-dressed, charismatic messenger would have been shot at any less.

It's about analysis, not about a popularity contest.

POSITIVE VALUES FOR THE FUTURE:

Subtance over form: The world is threaten by *empty suits* - people who have learned to mimic the mannerisms and dress of broad-minded, highly-skilled leaders. It is not hard: conservative haircut, reasonably good dental work, slacks from Banana Republic or Zara, whichever shirt and tie combo works for your corporate culture. Cliches are easy too, just use the following phrases: *market share, brand building, the world is flat[28], the new normal, do more with less, etc.* If you do this and nothing else, you can pretty much guarantee yourself a middle class existence in many countries. It would likely be better if we forbade haircuts and shaving and only allowed people to wear t-shirts and jeans in which they would feel comfortable painting their houses - then we could focus on the wisdom of what came out of their mouths instead of judging the easily available material trappings of upper-middle class professionals.

---

[27] *"Grabowiczsky," you see.*

[28] *For about five years there, anytime there was a moment of silence, some corporate person would fill the void by saying, "Uh...the world is flat!" apropos of absolutely nothing.*

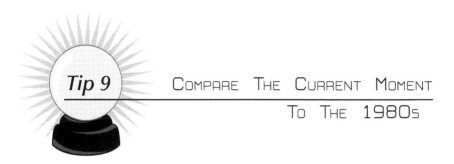

Tip 9

COMPARE THE CURRENT MOMENT TO THE 1980s

Repeat after me: "We tried it once in the 80s... it didn't work." This one phrase will protect you from thinking about everything about the future that sounds really disturbing.

In fact, EVERYTHING you see is just like the 1980s[29], with the minor exceptions of geopolitical situation, demographics, free availability of decades of cheap oil ahead, computer processing power, the prevailing assumptions of young people, and a few other differences.

- Searching for a digital content strategy? Ah, forget it - remember that time we recorded a bunch of audio products for sale and ended up with stacks and stacks of unused vinyl records? Boy, those were hard to store and we never made our money back.

- Worried about peak oil? Don't forget, we had that gas shortage

---

[29] *A notable exception to this rule is if you feel like starting an occupation in Afghanistan. Even though that was catastrophically attempted by a major power in the 1980s, I see no reason that you couldn't try the same thing in the present day with a considerably better result. .*

from OPEC in the 1970s, and even got nervous about more shortages in the 1980s - but hey, they never materialized! So I'm sure that there will be plenty of oil left despite minor new consumers such as all of China and all of India, the exhaustion of the Cantarell oil fields, etc.

• People have been caterwauling about the environment since the 1980s, and see, it didn't break.

You see, if it didn't happen in the thirty years between 1980 and 2010, it probably won't come to pass between 2010 and 2040, either.

>>>>>>>

The future intelligence view: The assumptions of the past do not match the future.

A couple of truisms about the psychology of leadership: First, people normally form their core beliefs and philosophies early in their careers, while they usually reach positions of true authority late in their careers. Second, we tend to project the assumptions that led to our success onto future generations, despite what ever differences in the world they will undoubtedly be experiencing. As a result, a distortion when thinking about the future tends to be quite common among executives - that what they learned in the 1980s is still valid and will be guiding the decisions of people in the future.

The main things that are distorted by hinging your assumptions on bygone decades:

1. *Limitations you remember may no longer be limitations.* (Processing power of computers, Communist empire dropping Iron Curtains and curtailing globalization)

2. *Things that were limitless may now be limited.* (Net energy exporters now net importers faced with peak oil, undeveloped suburban land no longer a convenient drive but half a day's drive away)

The chief value of futurism is not accurate predictions, but the exploration of unchallenged assumptions. While predicting who is going to win the World Cup is difficult, it is probably even tougher to explore the architecture of what we assume to be true about the past, present, and future. This is one reason not to blame people and bureaucracies for failing to naturally perceive the future - unless you take time and effort to examine your assumptions about what is next, you will automatically base decisions on information that could be out of date.

Let's create a picture of the future based on unexamined assumptions:

The forecast: *Distribution and logistics systems will work in a similar manner in the decades to come. Rail and trucking will take up roughly the same market share in 2030.*

The assumption: *We will have tons of cheap oil to fuel such a system - after all, I have never once faced a real change in the stability of oil prices since ascending to senior management in the late 1980s.*

Now, let us unpack those very assumptions, common to many decision makers, when thinking about energy availability in the decades to come. One common technique is to use forecasts from subject matter experts and compare these to our own assumptions. In this case, I will draw from forecasts by the U.S. Energy Information Administration and the International Energy Agency, both considered reputable sources.

In the first forecast by the EIA, we see that the mega-fields that produce the lion's share of global energy supply are set to drop off precipitously in the decades to come. We see also a huge chunk of that supply forecast to be filled by "Crude oil: fields yet to be developed or found."[30] Let us assume that there is at least a slight chance that not all of this extra oil will be found. Add to this a rapid increase in demand coming from India and China. These are fairly conservative estimates of both supply and demand - and still, price would be likely to fluctuate if not skyrocket.

Maybe rail and barge traffic might be a *teensy bit* more attractive if the world is looking at a whopping $250 per barrel of oil. The logistical system for nearly every activity in society would be upended. Trucks would be a terribly inefficient means of transporting goods. The structure of

---

[30] *Please think about how insane that kind of assumption is for a moment. .*

World oil production by type in the New Policies Scenario

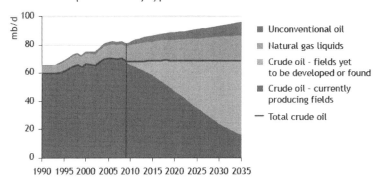

Global oil production reaches 96 mb/d in 2035 on the back of rising output of natural gas liquids & unconventional oil, as crude oil production plateaus

Change in oil demand by region in the 450 Scenario compared with 2008

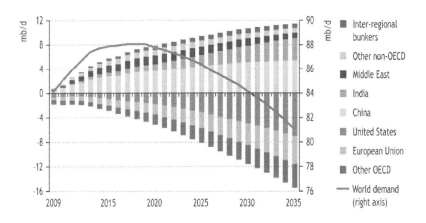

Oil demand peaks at 88 mb/d before 2020 & falls to 81 mb/d in 2035, with a plunge in OECD demand more than offsetting continuing growth in non-OECD demand

cities would be horribly mismatched to coming realities, and retail would undergo tectonic shifts.

Not exactly like what we saw between 1980 and 2010, is it?

Another set of unexamined assumptions in America right now concerns immigration. Most people do not realize it, but economic powerhouses usually depend on a reliable stream of talent coming from other countries to provide inspiration, insight, and raw skills to local industry. The medical world, for example, relies somewhat heavily on doctors and nurses wanting to leave their home countries for a putatively improved standard of living in the United States, Canada, Europe, and Australia. Back in the 1980s, many places with strong educational systems - Latin America being a good example - produced smart, talented individuals who wanted nothing more than to get the hell away from the military coups and calamities resulting from their nation's position as chess pieces in the Cold War. Ergo, can you perform an EKG? Can you provide ICU nursing care? Then you're going to get out of Bogotá as fast as possible into the welcoming environs of suburban New Jersey or the San Fernando Valley. Sure, the music is crap, and good luck ordering hot chocolate with melted cheese in it[31] without getting completely bizarre looks - but at least they aren't kidnapping non-mafia business leaders and killing judges in the streets.

Fast forward to the present day. India has substantial opportunity for top talent. Latin America is considerably more peaceful than in decades past, meaning many fewer reasons to escape at all cost to some colder northern climate with worse music and people in a rush all the time. And meanwhile, places like the United States have increased cost of living while keeping real wages flat. You will be paying three to five times more for a house than you would have in 1980, two and a half times for education. It's just not the same deal it was.

Imagine then, you are America's medical schools in the 1990s. Faced with the era of new health maintenance organizations (HMOs) which exist to control cost, you identify "time with doctors" as one of the chief costs. A fantastic new idea for shaping the strategic future of United States healthcare emerges - how about if we reduce the number of doctors we train so that there is a natural scarcity and we don't spend as much on doctors? Great idea!

---

[31] *"Chocolate con queso" - I swear Colombians love this, and they swear that it's good. The stuff to cherish is "sancocho" soup, which is the best hangover cure on earth. So I'm told.*

And so that's what they did, reduced the number of medical school spots and residencies a decade or so before the Boomers began their mass exodus from the field of medicine, as demand for healthcare shot up, and as the United States lost major ground in attractiveness for foreign medical graduates. Today, it is expected that by 2020 America will be short 200,000 doctors and 800,000 nurses - unlike, for example, the years of 1980 - 2010.

There is a reason we have assumptions - sometimes you just have to take things for granted. Imagine how difficult life would be if you got up every morning and took absolutely every experience as fresh, new, exciting, and undetermined. You wouldn't make it out of your kitchen - you would be stuck contemplating just WHAT exactly might be in those cereal boxes, whether eggs really do turn into tasty omelets when heat is applied, just how pans work, et cetera. We need to assume in order to function every day. That said, when we go to study the future, we can use the moment to examine our most cherished assumptions, even those that served us in good stead since the beginning of our careers.

POSITIVE VALUES FOR THE FUTURE:

Sweeping historical vision - There is no way to understand the future without at least considering how history has affected regimes and organizations of the past. That means going well beyond your early career as the "distant past" and actually understanding the transitions of several cycles throughout history. Kondratieff did pioneering work on this, as did Schumpeter, allowing people to see economies as cycles of forty to sixty years, giving a profoundly more insightful look at how our world is changing. Reading Roman, Greek, Persian, or Chinese history will also give a sense of rise and fall, of dynasties, of fate. Some moments are special. The world of the 1980s to now is a period with few analogues in history, and may not make a good comparison for the future. You can only know that if you have other eras in mind for comparison.

Get some Pliny the Elder on iBooks, I guess.

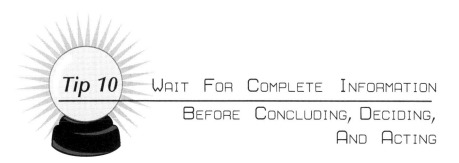

Tip 10 — WAIT FOR COMPLETE INFORMATION BEFORE CONCLUDING, DECIDING, AND ACTING

As you may have heard, predicting the future is about learning things before they happen, perchance to make a decision in advance of that future becoming the present. Decisions, as we all know, require the highest level of intellectual preparedness if they are to influence the gigantic bureaucracies we have taken pains to create over the past several decades.

As you know from tip five, **we are men of science!** Before deciding if something is significant enough to distract us from our holy work of influencing this quarter's numbers, we absolutely require quantification, spreadsheets, satellite imagery, genetic codes, a series of executive video podcasts from the Economist, Forbes, Bloomberg, and Highlights magazine, no more than a dozen syndicated reports from MarketPlatitudesToGo.com, and tarot readings from some of Hollywood's best card-based prognosticators. As you know, we at Hornsdog Partners recommend that all decisional data adhere to the standards that are incumbent with our 65th degree blackbelts in Nine Sigmoid X-treme Quality™ down to the 0.00000000000000001th dimension,

Only once these data sets are collected, alphabetized, converted to PowerPoint slides, exported to PDF files, arranged by color code and checked throughly by error-sniffing dogs can we know that some future forces are certain enough to act on, or more dangerously, discuss with our colleagues instead of opining about the upcoming sales conference.

>>>>>>>

The future intelligence view: If you wait for quantitative, absolutely authoritative polished information, you will go out of business before it arrives.

Making careful, data-dependant decisions is a good idea, especially when you are dealing with, say, a $100 billion dollar company with 43,000 employees, or say, a naval force with 250 warships all requiring thirty years of head-start to build and then billions of dollars of supply chain once they are in operation. These organizations have neither the size nor the agility of start-ups, and changes to their operations may have deep and unintended consequences. Getting the data is always a good idea before going ahead with decisions.

The reason this is called *future intelligence* is that, like in all intel assessments, you collect the best information available about the future, analyze it using the best techniques, and then you make a decision *still clouded in uncertainty*. **If we're talking about future megatrends, you will never have enough data to make you feel nice and comfortable until it is too late.**

Still, many organizations do not treat future trends as legitimate until they have all the trappings of modern, metrics-based management - reams of pointillistically filled out Excel spreadsheets, complete pricing information, the names of every company and person involved.

Peak oil? I need more data to really know exactly how much more its going to cost to keep our delivery trucks running.

Climate change? The jury is still out on just how many degrees of warming we're talking.

Aging populations? It's not certain how many people will retire and when, nor do we know exactly how much extra healthcare they might use.

You cannot even get complete data about things that have *already happened* such as sales and manufacturing - those numbers are often recreated with a certain level of inaccuracy despite our best efforts, in mammoth resource management and accounting software packages. So forget about getting that same level of easy-to-chart data for the strategic threats that will mean the fate of the organization.

One observation I have made over fifteen years of intelligence work, if it makes you feel any better - *intelligence is always wrong, it's just a question of by how much*. I know this may seem like a strange admission from someone who allegedly sells such services, but I do not believe this undercuts the *raison d'être* of the field. If you have a group study of *any* event in the world external to our organizations, it is limited in several critical ways. One way or another, you have a finite number of researchers, not more than ten people in the vast majority of cases. Those people are limited to reading things, usually on the Internet, and to calling people they either already know or find...on the Internet. No doubt if you have competent analysts, they have identified several of the major sources on whatever topic, have downloaded the reports, interviewed the thoughtleaders, arranged everything in as a pretty a document as possible. They may even at this point know more than any other group of people currently living about what is going on in the given subject.

There is no way this can be a completely accurate representation of the real-time events of a universe that is behaving on a quantum scale we can scarcely comprehend. The best we can do is cast a ray of light on the darkness, a ray full to the brim with observational bias, ignorance, and limited wisdom. There is no way that intelligence of any quality can be objectively true in the sense of Platonic ideals and universal truth.

And yet, this is vastly preferable to not doing it at all. There are important things to be learned from even imperfect attempts at intelligence, so long as we follow a rigorous and intellectually-honest methodology. What we learn may not result in the long-form, hard data sets expected by much of modern management. Yet it is no excuse for not looking out at the future, deriving insights, and leading an organization.

POSITIVE VALUES FOR THE FUTURE:

Courage: Yes, leading organizations into a complex and uncertain future is a gamblers game. Betting millions on a potential opportunity? Spending extra money to give your organization another option in case the future turns hostile? You could be sticking your neck out, wasting money, risking ridicule. Then again, when it is a guy like Jorma Ollila, worried about the Soviet collapse harming the diversified and dependent Nokia, when you bet the farm of mobile telephony, they call you a visionary. If you're betting with the fates of the future, you will need a healthy dose of courage. Then again, that is what we expect from leaders, is it not?

Tip 11

RELY ON TECHNOLOGY AND
BUSINESS, IGNORE CULTURE
SOCIETY PHILOSOPHY

C ulture is what losers do in their time off, which is plentiful because they are losers. Look, the world is about cash-money, big numbers, and bling. The only culture that counts is pop culture. The only pop culture that counts is making money right now for a corporation. The pop culture that counts is created by existing famous people[32], not newcomers with "talent." Worrying about art and singing and cooking, or whatever, is fine in your spare time, but the wise executive will focus on information that will actually drive ones and zeros.

Culture is fine for when you take your spouse on a much deserved trip to Paris or Florence to look at paintings by dead Italians. But it's technology that makes the Industrialized World great. We put a man on the moon. We put Hot Pockets in America's microwaves. We put granite countertops everywhere and video games into cellphones all around the world. Until there's a "philosophy" column on a balance sheet, let me show you a handy guide for the kinds of information you

---

[32] *By "famous people" I mean their staff of non-paid interns, you should know how this works by now.*

should consider in your reflections on the future:

In: Nanotech, telepresence, bioengineering, Second Life, 8G wireless, face-recognition technologies, derivatives, short sales, Forex, multi-level marketing

Out: Books, ideas, myths, logic, sentiment, spirit

>>>>>>>

The future intelligence view: The future is defined by far more than business alone.

Humans beings are creatures driven by myth, by spirit, by deep emotion. In order to give structure to enormous global enterprises our managerial techniques do much to overcome some of the more random, emotional elements in our collective behavior. However, when thinking about the future, one should never believe that management and bureaucratic institutions can outmatch the depth of the human spirit when it comes to shaping what is next for us all.

Futurism is entirely a social science. Even though financial projections and technology assessments all involve comfortably left-brained, hard numbers types of analysis, we are talking about forecasting the behavior of *people* here. I do not know if you have noticed that *we are pretty irrational more often than not*. There are seven billion of us running around, inventing stuff, growing crops, speaking languages, sending people to the moon, starting wars (a lot), starting religions, killing people who started *other* religions, blowing housing bubbles, colonizing other people's stuff, enslaving people, writing pop music, manufacturing iPods, holding a genocide here and there...you get the idea. There are some themes often drawn together after the fact, but while happening it is a fascinatingly chaotic mess of instinct, knowledge, superstition, culture, alcohol, reaction, overreaction and poetry.

I think I know why we leave the messy side to the philosophers and singer-songwriters and attempt to claim the logical, quantifiable side of the world as leaders of large organizations. It's harder to claim authority if you admit what a mêlée the whole thing really is. The only problem with that approach is that if you want to bend the chaotic nature of humanity to your will, you must be equally interested in the matters of the human spirit that defy easy classification.

Let's look at some major events in history that upended the world which might have been exceedingly difficult to forecast through structural trends alone.

The American and French Revolutions - Find me an 18th Century businessman who would have laid even money on the English New World and the French Old World defeating their respective masters, and I'll show you someone who was probably buying Dutch tulip bulbs high and selling them low.[33] All the stirringly patriotic stories of ferociously motivated and competent American resistance were written in *retrospect*. At the time, it was much more a story of a group of dissatisfied English colonists organizing some half-trained regiments and barely-disciplined militias against the most powerful military force on the planet.

And what of their brothers in revolt over in France? Toothless, bootless peasants rising up against one of the richest, best equipped and most established regimes in the world, all while barely able to keep from starving to death in one of the worst years of crop shortage in history.

The fuel to the fire of liberty was as cultural as it was economic and political. The scientific revolution was illuminating minds around Europe, giving rise to brand new fields of scientific inquiry - physics, chemistry, and biology. Where medieval Europe was ruled by absolutists who burned all social and political critics under the banner of heresy, the Renaissance finally moved the mind and spirit of the people toward ideal principles in the tradition of the Classical Age. By the time the Scientific Revolution came about, it provided a methodology that could challenge assumptions and settle arguments. The era of being able to declare truth from on high and torture all of those who challenged it was quickly being surrounded by a world that made its advances based on what was universally true, demonstrably correct.[34]

Were the American colonists fighting because they were willing to

---

[33] *Which was 150 years prior to those events, but y'know I just don't have any examples of Ponzi schemes in the late 1700s off the top of my head. Work with me.*

[34] *Sad to see this part go in the other direction these days...*

die over the concept of "taxation without representation?" Perhaps. Did the French start the Première République because they were starving while the fops of Louis XVI's court cavorted at Versailles? Sure. But one can argue that beneath the surface, inflaming the human spirit, was the irresistible power of empirical reason, challenging despotism and injustice by its very nature. How could one human brain deal with science rapidly decoding the mysteries of existence while also accepting orders from tyrants who were faking a commitment to anything that approached reason?

The end of the Soviet Union - There is no question, the Soviet Union was spending 50% of its GDP on military spending to match the deficit-insensitive arms race of Reagan's Pentagon. The Soviet Union had become a nation of gleaming MiG 29s, fearsome intercontinental nuclear warheads, and very little else. Factories in disrepair. Farms of broken tractors and fallow fields. Empty stores. The economics of the Soviet Union were no doubt a key factor in the decline of the empire.

But why did the empire crumble from within? Might it have had something to do with the relentless onslaught of images of cultural advancement from west of the Iron Curtain? Could it have been blue jeans? Pepsi? Stephen Spielberg movies? There needs to be some central logic to any political movement. Communism originally had this going for it. In the 1920s, the proletariat was not exactly thriving under the Tsar's system of feudal serfdom, and so while the Russian Revolution may also be interpreted as "new boss, same as the old boss," there was at least a good reason to *try* the new boss. Plus, Marx promised them that they would "win" history. Sounds great, let's revolt and get some gulags going!

But culturally, what did the latter communist system promise the Poles, the Estonians, the Czech, or even the Russians themselves? There is only so much propaganda one can create to counter the awesome impact of the occasional arrival of black market rock records and comfortable denim. Sure, perhaps the capitalist dogs kept workers in the ghettos of their factory cities to starve, but *man* are these Levi's good looking. And have you heard the latest Huey Lewis and the News? Their new album *Sports* rocks your Kalashnikov off, Comradeski.

It is perhaps no wonder, then, why most of the national intelligence analysts of the occidental world failed to see the imminent collapse of the communist superpower. While structural trends indicated a certain amount of weakness, it was impossible to truly calculate the fatigue of the people of the USSR and the seduction of Western progress. The Defense Intelligence Agency can count missile silos and tanks, but it is unable to track the evolution of a myth that guides people to cooperate as a military and economic adversary.

I'm in love with my car, got a feel for my automobile

Management in the age of globalization has become increasingly abstract. This is not without good reason, as the coordination of such massively complex activity needs to be reduced into repeatable, quantifiable tasks. While this works for putting together automobiles from parts made by thousands of suppliers, it ignores the personal aspect of organizations by its very nature. But what about tracking how people *feel* about automobiles? You cannot look at the history of the car business in the United States without considering the awesome power that culture played in its domination of the industry. The Beach Boys wrote a song about a Little Deuce Coupe, about the tragedy of Daddy taking the T-Bird away, of Little Hondas. Who the hell writes rock songs about blow molded plastics? Did the Beatles say, "Baby, you can use my Hoover to clean your apartment?" Did the Doors sing, "Come on baby, light my energy efficiency GE fluorescent bulbs?"

Car advertisements of the 1940s were cerebral entreaties to a man's scientific appreciation of engine design and carburetor quality. Since that time, the majority of car ads for U.S. brands feature cowboys making out with bald eagles at football games while Bruce Springsteen wrestles Bob Seeger.[35] These are homages not only to the relative toughness of pickup trucks, as much as paeans to a nation that tore up the way cities had been made for 10,000 years, to make way for a lifestyle that puts the automobile first. The car is a deep-seated story of man's dominance and its myth is cultural, economic, political, and sexual.

Imagine, then, if the American culture after the Second World War became more about group cohesion and less about consumption and wide open spaces. There might have been billions spent on trolley cars and

---

[37]Americans: I have $500 if you can tell me what the song "Like a Rock" is actually about WITHOUT looking up the lyrics on Wikipedia. It's not trucks. Send responses to P.O. Box 63155 Saint Louis, MO 63163.

bicycles instead of four-wheel drive nature-conquering trucks. Holy cow, we could have been the *Dutch*.

A sophisticated cultural understanding of the world is far from the domain of art appreciation professors at the junior college. These trends are every bit as much about billion dollar decisions as the spot price of copper.

POSITIVE VALUES FOR THE FUTURE:

Holistic thinking - Your analysis may ultimately need to be compressed to a few images and bullet points (the legacy of the dreaded mental cage known as PowerPoint), but it must contain a universe of information about the beauty and mystery of the world around us. If you are in business, you are selling to people. People are complex, unfathomable, ever changing, enigmatic, elusive. How they change, in all of the glorious mystery implied, is your business as an analyst. It will be your job as a professional to relate a holistic worldview into whichever metrics your organization uses to measure future performance. Especially in our spread-sheet mad managerial culture, this will be a tall order - but, hey, if you want to understand the future, this is what is required. Hopefully it is more fulfilling and fun than rows and columns of numbers as a form of consolation.

Trendiness - I generally abhor the shallowness of modern "trend watchers" masquerading as prophets of something more meaningful. Usually, I don't care what kinds of sneakers the kids in Brooklyn are wearing while we are drawing down water tables on four continents and China is reaching strategically into Africa with long-term contracts that will guarantee them access to raw materials for the next century of manufacturing. And true, I often say that coal is more important than shiny gadgets, that ball bearings are more important than 3D televisions. Having said that, *you cannot ignore the zeitgeist at the expense of the long-term, either*. Yes, if you stop the flow of iPhones it does not matter as much as if you stopped the flow of natural gas. But how can you ignore the bigger implications of the smartphone zeitgeist - that we have become a people who can maintain relationships digitally, virtually anywhere? It leads to all kinds of implications:

- social isolation in the real world
- the rise of geolocation marketing
- mobile banking in Africa
- microloans for impoverished communities
- police accountability through camera phones
- real-time surveillance of a population

While these are big trends that last for decades, they play out in ways big and small right here, right now, where we live. And many a marketer has figured out how to turn this into big money.

Apple comes to mind. They understand the long-term extremely well, and they craft business models accordingly. They have remade the music industry in their image, redefined upper-end, service-oriented experiential retail, and seen a world of information technology beyond the desktop and laptop. *And* they also time their product releases down to the week to choose the ideal moment when their goods should hit the public consciousness. Massive global supply chains dovetail with up-to-the-minute trendiness. Judge for yourself the results.

Tip 12   Say You are Looking Out 20
Years But Study Today Instead

N othing sounds better than announcing that you are planning to study the future. This works especially in local, state, provincial and federal government, but can work equally well for private sector concerns. Announce in lavish fashion that you are, as opposed to the rest of the time, FINALLY going to consider the long-term implications of what you are doing.

Pause for effect, to allow people to cheer for you or for them to don sunglasses so they can stare at an intellect bright and wise enough to predict the future. You are, after all, why the swarthy people underneath you are going to WIN.

Now that's out of the way, select your team of visionaries. Now you can get down to the serious business of discussing today's projects and which of them are most likely to lead to the preferred scenario of us being number one in the future. Take special care not to let any scary information about the uncertain world creep in and disturb your meditation about the current situation. See Tip #2 if you need further inspiration.

When you are done, write a florid document about your new mission statement to be number one in everything by 20-whatever. Mention the wisdom of the current strategy, and if there's time, throw in a few platitudes about meeting the "challenges of the future" to assure the good people that you're not all Pollyannaish. After all, it will be hard work doing the same things as you're doing now, only for longer.

>>>>>>>

The future intelligence view: Faux foresight is more harmful than none at all.

I used to think that the worst thing a group of leaders could do would be to engage in a rigid, short-term mentality when making decisions. After all, the future is out there, bla bla bla, opportunities and threats, you should look at the future, see footnote.[36] Now, I think that it is probably worse to say you are thinking about the future while simply rehashing the same debates about the current situation.

In an ideal world, every organization would incorporate the discipline of *future intelligence* into all of their operations, all of their decisions. Until we reach such nirvana, futures studies tend to happen periodically, requiring a certain amount of convincing from the rest of the bureaucracy that is engaged with the day-to-day fight of managing a world in transition. It takes energy to get a group inspired by the notion of thinking ahead. So it's all the more a tragedy if we look at the future and it is wasted on all-too-common bickering over the current dilemma.

A couple of government reports come to mind.[37] One was the study of the future of a region. They announced in florid press conferences how, "Yes, Now We Are Going to Study the Future!" There were parades, juggling monkeys, a month of feasts, lotus petals dispersed to float on all lakes and rivers in the region. The project was to last many months. The methodology was to ask various members of the region *what they*

---

[36] *It's all in* Future, Inc.: How Businesses Can Anticipate and Profit from What's Next, *as well as about a thousand other books on the topic. No need to rehash it here.*

[37] *NOTE: Neither I nor Competitive Futures were involved in the production of these projects.*

wanted the future to look like in twenty years. At the end of the many months, the final document was released. The people had spoken and their desires were clear.

Clear desire for the future: More education! More public transit! Free healthcare! Curb global warming!.

Conclusion: We should go do that.

Unmentioned: Aging populations, shrinking private sector jobs growth, loss of agribusiness sector, crippling future entitlements, potential technologies and approaches to actually achieve the goals set out through some sort of a tax base.

On every other page of the final report were lengthy congratulations from local and international political leaders thanking the intrepid intellectual voyagers for their important study of the future. After all, their discoveries surely ranked with Magellan, Pasteur, Watson & Crick - that people want better schools, affordable healthcare, more fuzzy puppies, lower taxes, awesomer televisions, and world peace. And that, y'know, we should go do that. By 2030. Or something.

Another report was an analysis of geopolitical trends through 2025. After millions of dollars in tax expenditures and the brain cells of countless analysts boiled by lakes of coffee, the radical future was judged to be the following:

- The world probably won't be like it has been since World War II.
- Russia will be corrupt.
- Nukes may fall into the hands of people we don't really trust.
- Climate change might be a big deal, kind of, in some places.
- The American economy might not be the only game in town.
- Oh, and we'll totally be off oil by 2025, and on some magic technology. Probably.

Well, that was exhilarating, wasn't it? That actually could have been a futures study from 1991, but it was published in 2008 not long after the financial system nearly collapsed a hole in the universe and sucked everyone into oblivion. The problem, aside from the fact that this was the product of professional analysts and not a high school geography class, is that the media reported these findings as if they were the pinnacle of the profession of foresight. If I were leading a world-class organization of stunning complexity, I am not sure that such insights would inspire me to engage in such a discipline. That is perhaps even worse than spending the majority of your time on tactical execution and only occasionally looking out at the future in a highly focused, useful way.

Faux foresight sullies the name of a discipline we need more and more as the world increases in complexity.

POSITIVE VALUES FOR THE FUTURE:

Intellectual rigor - If we want a culture that produces a sustainable, prosperous, healthy, just world that can think about the future, our efforts in foresight must be of the utmost intellectual quality. By its own uncertain nature, foresight permits and often requires creative visions of what could come next. There is a fine line between a creative vision based on reliable data and simply making stuff up off the top of your head. Many people cross this line while associating themselves with the analytical discipline of professional futurists.[38] The unfortunate reaction of the public is to think of *all* future thinking as illegitimate. Badly conceived, useless futures studies achieve largely the same effect. Studies of the future, to be credible must go beyond the rigor employed in all other management disciplines.

Self-criticism - There are many, many pitfalls when you attempt a study of the future for which someone is paying, and after which important decisions will be made. It is all too easy to fall into a trap that dooms your study to self-regarding, useless refuse. It is important to create a culture during the study where you stop and say, "Hey, is this *any* good? Are we actually getting at the heart of the matter?" You need room in this kind of reflection to question yourself, to make it OK, to create a truly creative environment. In a world where people are pilloried for mistakes - even in this world of innovation, moving cheese, and expecting the unexpected - you must counter these tendencies if you want the freedom to study the future in a way that is strategically useful.

---

[38] *One word: Singulatarians.*

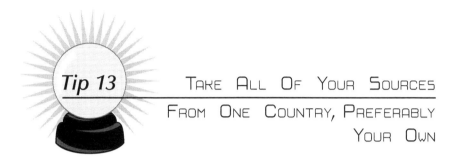

Tip 13 — Take All Of Your Sources From One Country, Preferably Your Own

If you start reading newspapers and academic research from around the world, this foresight thing is going to get out of hand in a hurry. First of all - foreign languages. Who has time for them? If something is worth knowing, it's worth putting in English.

Also, you get the added bonuses of being able to keep any infantile domestic political biases completely in tact if you only take information from your home country. Imagine trying to study cultural trends in both the United States AND Turkey at the same time. You'd have to try to recreate America's monumentally childish left-right narrative while attempting to deal with the fact that Turkey's left wing is militaristic and nationalistic but also secular. And then you'd have to understand that in the country's culture war, abortion and prostitution are totally legal, but people lose their minds over wearing head scarves in public buildings.

If you're a serious leader, consider the future as it appears in your own language. If you are interested in other cultures, watch the Travel Channel, take some vacations, and consider a French course at the local community college. Otherwise, get serious.

>>>>>>>

The future intelligence view: You cannot study the global future while ignoring most of the globe.

This theme is mostly aimed at the famously monolingual American readers here, but it can be true for the myopic nationalists in every culture. It is tempting, but very dangerous, to base all analysis of the future on trend information published in your mother tongue.

As razões para esta são realmente completamente simples. Aunque 66% de la población del mundo tiene conocimiento basico de dos idiomas, hablar al nivel professional es todavía difícil. Donc, l'on aura naturellement une tendance à compter sur les sources que l'on trouve dans sa langue maternelle. Het is natuurlijk moeilijker informatie om te underzoeken in andere talen. アジア言語はにさらにもっと困難である. 全球化是复杂的.[39]

Still, if you are a global business with thousands of employees, difficulty is no excuse not to have analysis taking place in multiple major foreign languages. In Europe, of course, this problem is solved fairly easily by hiring any Dutch or Swiss person over the age of 18.[40] For other nations, you can begin your path to multinational, cosmopolitan, insightful analysis by HIRING ONE OF THE MANY FOREIGN LANGUAGE MAJORS WHO HAS NO IDEA WHAT TO DO WITH THEIR DEGREE![41] Sorry for the all-caps, but the resources are out there to begin building analytical

---

[39] *Sorry, that's Portuguese, Spanish, French, Dutch, Japanese and Chinese, respectively, for "The reasons for this are actually quite simple. Even though fully 66% of the world's population has working knowledge of two languages, reaching professional-level proficiency is difficult outside of one's mother tongue. Thus, we naturally tend to count on sources we find in our own language. It is naturally more difficult to search for information in foreign languages. Asian languages are even more difficult for foreigners. Globalization is complex."*

[40] *I have never met a person from the Netherlands or Switzerland who wasn't fluent in seventeen languages and able to freestyle rap in six of them. In the case of the Dutch, a particularly insightful man from Groningen once explained his nation's language prowess by saying, "Hey, a few hundred years ago, we tried to take over the world and make everybody speak Dutch. It didn't work. So we're learning your languages now. It's only fair." They are a pragmatic people.*

[41] *University of Vermont, Bachelors of Arts in Romance Languages and Business Administration - HOLLA*

departments with a truly global scope. But why bother, you ask?

The greatest thing about data sources from other countries is the diverse assumptions automatically included in their analysis. Let's say you are coming from an American background, with its own special authorities and media providing a very particular view of the world indeed. What will non-American sources provide you, almost no matter what the subject? It is really all about ingrained assumptions:

- For Asians, the future isn't always about a happy ending.
- For Europeans, it's not all about business or about being number one.
- If you're in South America, the future may be more about brand-new vistas than the maintenance of past glories.

From a tactical intelligence perspective, here is another reason to love foreign sources: the public relations services that maintain language discipline in describing a company's activities are rarely global in scope and controlled from a central location. The craft of PR is often choosing exactly the right words to achieve a certain image in the mind of the public. If you have ever studied foreign languages or done anything resembling technical-level translation, you know that most words have NO exact counterpart in another language. Every word in a given translation has at least some nuance that distinguishes it from similar terms in the target language. Practically, this means that you cannot enforce strict language discipline between countries, and organizations are likely to release different information in every country, giving a more complete picture of their operations. While this is a particularly useful tip for competitor intelligence practices, the broader value is applicable to every analytical discipline. You will simply learn more by seeking out information in multiple languages, even if you do not go that deep.

Either way, it is impossible to effectively know what's coming in a superconnected world system without a direct connection to different cultures through their native languages. Make a liberal arts major happy and hire one today with language skills. Or your business will go bankrupt in the next four months.[42]

POSITIVE VALUES FOR THE FUTURE:

---

[42] *Fellow liberal arts types: I'm trying here, back me up and take some classes in accounting to meet the world half way.*

Cosmopolitanism - There is no way to understand the future without a deep and abiding commitment to understanding the amazing diversity of thought around the world. Values, impressions, assumptions, dreams, obligations - these are all different depending on the culture. If you are trying to forecast future human behavior, you need a sense of just how diverse that behavior can be. Otherwise, you will almost certainly project your deep cultural biases onto all of your forecasts and implications since you will not be able to really imagine people acting any other way.

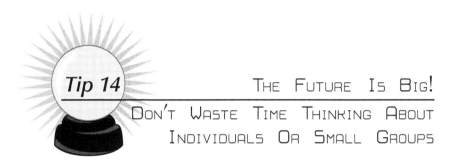

Tip 14

THE FUTURE IS BIG! DON'T WASTE TIME THINKING ABOUT INDIVIDUALS OR SMALL GROUPS

You may occasionally be tempted to consider the actions of entrepreneurs, small nations, individuals when considering the future. This is a major trap. Look, if those people were really worth considering, they would have been bought out a long time ago by some company looking to unload some cash reserves into a favorable strategic equity positioning.

This theorem can be connected to those who are struggling, or might have struggled in the past.

Look at dinosaurs - they were big, and see how many of their bones we find everywhere. That's how important they were!

>>>>>>>

97

The future intelligence view:

We did this trend in number three already. Clearly, Egon's publishers wanted him to stretch this book out. After all, books with 250 pages but only 50 pages of ideas are BETTER than books of 100 pages with 80 pages of ideas. And you can jack the prices on them.

POSITIVE VALUES FOR THE FUTURE:

Brevity - Say what you need to say and no more.

Tip 15 — Take It Personally! Make Sure Your Ego Is The Star Of All Visions Of The Future, One In Which YOU WIN

This insight should be obvious. After all, who wants to hear about a future in which they are not superstars? A future in which the company or even the country isn't dominant? Unacceptable! Second place is the first loser!

You were placed in a position of leadership to make the future huger and awesomer. Make certain that if you are going to spend the time to describe the future, your scenarios make you come out looking like an even bigger superstar. This means if anybody is describing a future in which you are not a winner of even greater global standing in zero-sum terms, they should be immediately administered massive doses of anti-depressants with a mood stabilizer chaser.

>>>>>>>

The future intelligence view: **Understand the emotional reaction of those affected by your work in foresight.**

We are dealing with human beings in all of this, and humans like to

WIN. Futurism and competitive intelligence exists because tomorrow, the winners and losers will be different than today. Also, foresight is critical to competitive analysis because nobody is guaranteed a stable position forever. Still, nobody *wants* to hear about things getting worse, they want to hear about how they will WIN. Nobody *wants* to hear that the company might lose standing on their watch, no matter what irresistible forces oppose them. Trade our corporate Gulfstream 5 intercontinental jet for the Gulfstream 3 that only travels *intra*continentally? Are you out of your mind?

Of course, people still *need* to hear these things. And of course, they will not like it. This psychological reality is particularly important when discussing change with leaders of today's organizations in a time of such fundamental shift across the board. Many of our institutions are the largest such bureaucracies ever to exist in history and the profits they produce are equally at an apex of hugeness. The industrial system and the modern society of nation-states that accompany it are, at the end of the day, a massive success. If you were dreaming of capitalistic industrial companies thriving, you may never have even dared to dream of things reaching the heights we have been witnessing in the last couple decades.

Of course, all good things come to an end. And if the strategic forces on the horizon are any indicator, it is unlikely the cheap-oil-fueled, suburban-housing-driven system of global finance capitalism will continue to grow, but instead now decompose as a new global system emerges. This means that numbers will stop going up. This means that a generation of managers taught to mindlessly press ahead for larger numbers at all costs will be shocked to see their only success metric become terribly difficult to reach. People are going to be disappointed.

The neurological background to this psychological behavior is quite telling. Neurobiologists will describe the different roles of the frontal lobe, the mid brain and the "lizard brain" in the behavior of people. Highly ordered thinking - the kind demanded for foresight - is located uniquely in the prefrontal cortex. The ability to form social bonds resides in the midbrain. And the basics of our "monkey rules" are found in the back of the brain. When you are feeling good about yourself and unthreatened, you are free to use your frontal lobe and have wonderful thoughts about the future. In times of tribulation, the frontal cortex becomes harder to engage, leaving you stuck in the midbrain, shoring up your social relationships to make sure that the tribe survives. But when the defecation hits the ventilation, you are headed for the lizard brain, which only has a few operations to manage:

- Defend territory
- Get mate
- Kill threat

When you are under extreme stress, your thoughts will naturally gravitate - according to observable laws of biology - toward fighting, screwing and killing anything that wants to give you less territory in which to hunt. Let us apply this tendency toward strategic thinking.

One of the reasons Hitler's Germany lost World War II was the Führer's absolute refusal in the later part of the war to let his armies retreat as much as a *meter* once they gained territory for *Großedeutschland*. Tactically, even if the armies forded a river and found themselves facing increased enemy resistance from fresh reinforcements, they were not allowed to retreat *at all* to a place where they might regroup and counterattack. *No retreat whatsoever, not even a meter.* This is, from a military perspective, completely stupid. From the lizard brain perspective, however, this is totally logical.

"Russians come. Threat. Expand territory. Ugh. Find mate. Get more territory. Forward, never back. Ugh."

See? If you are unable to take a broad view of the situation due to stress, your only options can be long on aggression and short on nuance. They are simpler to understand, though likely less successful than their broad, sophisticated counterparts.

Picture then the CEO, in a recession and in a massive global transformation, being informed that he[43] may need to retreat to a business model that will be more likely to return profit, but at a smaller topline revenue than previous years. Let us take record company CEOs as an example. Most people at this apex moment in history want to act like their forebears of the industrial system and *expand territory*. Sadly, it just might not be an option. If you are in a think tank analyzing the industry, this may

---

[43] *I could use a "he/she" formula here, but I find that the female gender has fewer issues with this kind of monkey-brained territorial aggression. You get a Queen Isabella now and then, but most of the female leaders of history were less likely to plow ahead on insane quests for land and treasure in defiance of all logic. Sorry guys, this is mostly our problem.*

be just another observation. If you are charged with the responsibility for thousands of employees and billions in capital, this may sound like ugly, harrowing news. Stressful news. You refuse to cede territory and begin suing your customers for breaching copyright law. Suing teenagers and cancer patients is long on aggression, short on nuance, nonsensical tactics. But from the lizard perspective, it makes ultimate sense to *protect territory* at all costs.

Bottom line: this is emotional business, no matter what your IQ is. **Nearly everybody you meet with a leadership position in business and government is smart.** If only we could get away with calling people "stupid" when they don't agree with us or do the right thing. Analysis is not just about being smart and right. It's about being able to reach people on levels both emotional and analytical, to help them, to broaden their minds. It is impossible to estimate how few people seem to grasp this fact. Perhaps we have just all taken too many standardized tests, we all think that we are being tested for the single right answer, and whoever gets it is the smartest. That's fine for multiple choice exams, but it has nothing to do with leading organizations into a complex and uncertain future. That is the territory of gut instinct, emotion, personal connection, destiny. It is psychology. This is almost never discussed and it is a crying shame.

If discussions of the future are to have any significant impact, we must embark on a journey to understand how people react emotionally to information, as well as rationally.

POSITIVE VALUES FOR THE FUTURE:

Process over content - When I started as a futurist, I honestly believed that my work was 90% information, 10% process. As a young man, I figured that all the world needed was the right answers delivered in a credible way and then the wisest, justest, awesomest, most profitable, cleanest, most sustainablest perfect decision would happen naturally. After working for more than a decade with almost exclusively smart, fair, hard-working, good people, I realize that information is hardly the most important part of the job. Affecting positive future change involves approximately 20% data and 80% process. It simply matters a great deal how the future is presented in order to move an individual to action, much less a bureaucracy involving thousands of them. This sophisticated understanding of human beings is a tall order. It takes humility and forbearance. And once again, so does being a good leader.

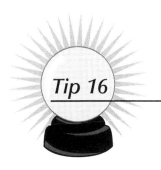

Tip 16 — NEVER MAKE COMPARISONS TO HISTORY! THOSE JERKS DIDN'T EVEN HAVE COMPUTERS!

We live in a time of genomic nanotech knuckle-top computing with built-in telepresence, obvious evidence that we live at the pinnacle of the human experience with no connection to our disgraceful failures of past centuries. Occasionally, when predictizing the future, some people will consider forecasts in terms of things that happened in some pre-telepresence era of carving naked guys into rocks. This kind of bizarre obsession with dead people and pointless things is clearly a sign of not wanting to predict the future and actually WIN.

Afghanistan is a great example of this. At the time of this printing, the United States is running a cleverly managed and wonderfully successful war there. You might say, "Wait a minute, that's not the same 'Graveyard of Empires' Afghanistan that inspired the Princess Bride quote about avoiding land wars in Asia, is it?" And yes, it is that very army-swallowing mass of rebel-infested, goat-scented caves and desolate boulder collections. And yes, a couple of empires might have been ground to a gruesome paste in those very mountains, such as every single one since Alexander the Great.

BUT - there are many great reasons not to compare what's happening there today to the distant past of the 1980s, as these depressed Luddite fools keep insisting.

Have you ever met anybody from the United States? Now, do they really have anything in common with Sir John Keane and Konstantin Chernenko? Of course not! None of those guys watched football, beat the Nazis, or participated in the greatest country in the history of countries. So, I ask you, what use is it pointing out that those men represented the greatest empires of their time, English and Russian respectively, both of which perceived themselves to be invincible? You might be tempted to continue the analysis to say, "Wow, it seems as if EVERYBODY gets their butt kicked in Afghanistan, even the biggest empires of their day." And naturally, what a trap this would be, since we know that history doesn't really provide patterns that can guide us for the future.

And thus, my accurate prediction that America would go on to crisp, glorious success in subduing Afghanistan, despite the utter failure of anybody doing this in the past 2500 years.

Also, if it's never worked before in history, assume that this is because the people who came before you are demonstrably stupid.

>>>>>>>

The future intelligence view: A study of the future is impossible without an appreciation of the past.

"The past isn't dead and buried - it isn't even the past." - William Faulkner

Sometimes I think the most dangerous phrase in the English language is *"But this time, it's different!"*[44] They say that the past repeats itself twice, first as tragedy, then as farce. The farcical aspect usually comes from the fact that people are repeating the past without even realizing it, mostly because they don't have enough knowledge of it to notice.

Here is the big trick in studying the future: distinguishing between that

---

[44] *Runners up: "No money down!" "Quantitative easing!" and "You're the father!"*

which is totally brand new and that which is a past reality with a new coat of paint slapped on.

Same old: Mothers love their children, city tension with rural areas, income disparity, new technology solving some problems and creating new ones, China and India dominating the majority of global GDP.[45]

Brand new: Genomic medicine, high-definition telepresence, grey populations dominating the world.

Look: We drive on roads the size of two horse's behinds, which we inherited from railroads, which they inherited from Roman roads designed for their chariots of the day. Our legal system traces back to the Forum in Rome. Some of our geopolitical tensions, say Western Europe and Iran, were called "Rome versus Parthia" 2000 years ago. The past has this amazing ability to stick around a very long time.

One of my favorite passages from antiquity is from a book of average rhetoric in the Athens assembly from two millennia ago. These transcriptions were not historically special orations, just a series of speeches from Athenians that showed what was on the mind of those who ran the city-state. My favorite speech is a lamentation about *"why is it that teachers are paid so little to assure the future of our people, while we heap adulation and money upon athletes?"* It seems that there are some issues we never quite manage to improve, even given a couple thousand years to think about them.

Some stories to remember about historical patterns: Every new information technology comes with a promise of world peace and ubiquitous, high quality, free education- and then we go ahead and use it for war, entertainment and pornography. And no, I'm not just referring to television and internet - those were the first uses of POTTERY. But let's skip past the bronze age to the 19th century.

Telegraph: While too clunky to provide education and far too dull to excel at entertainment or pornography, the telegraph was expected to end war because now, there would be ample communication between governments to be able to defuse tensions.

Actual uses: Troop coordination, creation of stock bubbles and depressions

---

[45] *Seriously, look it up.*

Radio: Still too boring for pornography, the radio was predicted to assure world peace and provide free education all over the world. Peace seemed inevitable because now we would be able to develop wonderful empathy for people all over the world, regardless of the physical or cultural distance, since we could talk to them so easily. Peace would also ensue from all world languages dwindling down to one or two major dialects, removing the differences between us. Moreover, now teachers could beam awesome education to the planet for free!

> *Actual uses: Coordination of bombers over cities, occasionally armed with nukes. Broadcast of Burns & Allen comedy hour, Glenn Miller concerts, and baseball play-by-plays.*

Television: By now, people were getting ever better at predicting world peace and free education from new technologies. Clearly, it was just the lack of a *picture* that was keeping radio back from delivering utopia. The rub with television was that the free education would lead to the end of ignorance and thus peace.

> *Actual uses: Stultifying entertainment and war propaganda, occasionally at the same time. EXCELLENT for pornography when combined with the VCR and Cinemax in the early 1980s.*

Internet: Clearly it was just the centralized broadcasting that was keeping radio and television from the peaceful educational heaven on earth that we have been promised. Now, the people of the world could beam free education and peace to each other over modems, in whatever the language!

> *Actual uses: Dot Com bubbles, online education, coordinating revolutions against dictators, videos of cats playing keyboards and Charlie biting his brother's finger, ignorant political debates, transmission of plans for making bombs out of household items. Unbelievably effective as vector for pornography, with as much as 37% of usage going for this purpose.*[46]

Who knows, maybe that peace and education technology we have been waiting for is right around the corner, but you cannot escape the fact that it is useful to know how these kinds of prognostications have worked out in previous decades.

---

[46] *"More than one third of web pages are pornographic" Optenet, June 16, 2010, viewed at http://www.optenet.com/en-us/new.asp?id=270*

Know the past and dare to make original mistakes.

POSITIVE VALUES FOR THE FUTURE:

Common humanity - The notion of appreciating history is coming up several times in Dr. Egon's work, so here is another angle. If you read enough history you don't see how truly strange people were, you see how *alike* we are across the ages. Since people started living in cities, we have been specializing labor, taxing the dickens out of each other, occasionally going to war with other people, making art, teaching our kids, overpaying athletes, criticizing politicians, thinking that the next generation is a bunch of lazy screw-ups, and more. Look into a bust of Julius or Augustus Caesar at a museum and you will find yourself staring at...an Italian guy. Yes, that particular Italian guy might have conquered Gaul, might have created a vast empire of marble where he found brick, but, at the end of the day, the guy looks like one of my uncles.[47] We do many things that are new and different and many, many things that are exactly the same. The soul of a great intelligence analyst is to be able to distinguish which is which as we look at the external world.

---

[47] *Actually, it's my friend Sam's uncle Carlucci Mazzariello who looks the most like the Caesars, though he has yet to conquer Gaul and Parthia.*

Tip 17 — WHATEVER YOU DO, DON'T INVITE YOUNG PEOPLE, POOR PEOPLE, ARTISTS OR ANY DIVERSE OPINIONS TO THE TABLE. MAKE SURE LEADERS ARE THE ONLY ONES IN THE DISCUSSION

People, as you know, are in positions of authority because they are, 99.9999% of the time, considerably smarter, wiser, and more perceptive than the rest of the people in the world. Thus, if you wan't to know the future, spend as little time as possible paying attention to the rabble. Maybe they have enough money and sophistication to buy some of your products, but the probability that they might have a point of view worth considering is somewhat less than the probability of somebody high-jumping over the Arc de Triomphe.[48]

>>>>>>>

The future intelligence view: Don't forget stakeholders.

With the rise of corporate social responsibility came a vocabulary word that has been in vogue amongst the broad-

---

[50]*Amérloques: C'est très grand, l'Arc de Triomphe, c'est pourquoi ça serait difficile de le sauter. Grosse bande d'imbéciles.*

minded: stakeholders. This word is just a syllable or two away from "shareholders," the really special people who provide capital to companies. But they are not the same. You see, stakeholders are the people who are also affected by the actions of an organization but have no direct bureaucratic connection with it. They often provide no money, have no regulatory authority, have power neither to improve or damage the situation - in other words, are pretty ignorable most of the time.

Grand plans created from the top designed to radiate downward are truly dependent on a social contract with those who *lack* power, and the ranks of the powerless appear to be growing. There has been a rapidly expanding global industrial system, yet ironically, more and more people are becoming disenfranchised from it. One of the critical problems of tomorrow will likely be global unemployment stemming from increasingly specialized market niches and robotic automation of a variety of jobs. There is no conspiracy going on, it's just what happens in a world of increasing worker productivity and better information technology. People are costly, and if you can replace cashiers with self-kiosks, there is a business case that supports doing so. If you can get rid of human workers in favor of manufacturing robots placed in a country with cheaper overhead, then that's a no-brainer decision as well. Ironically, this is all happening during a period of record crop yields due to biotechnology, satellite information systems, and petroleum-supported agriculture. Hence the world has been increasing in population at the same time. More people, fewer jobs.

Eventually, there will be so many people lacking the requisite skills to join the economy that there could be major instability. Consider how many of these disenfranchised masses are going to be young and energetic, especially in the places with the lowest standards of living. Without investment in a given system, they will have very little motivation not to disrupt it. While it may be tempting to say that this sounds more like a problem for some non-profit, it is important to remember that in this globally-interconnected economy, it is amazing how fast unrelated things tend to impact our bottom lines.

POSITIVE VALUES FOR THE FUTURE:

Inclusiveness - If you want a global business, you get a globe with it. Keep your ears open to see the future from a variety of points of view inside and outside of your organization. You will get a special look into future threats and opportunities.

Tip 18

Start With The Conclusions In Mind And Push All Information Toward Them

Look, my colleagues, we all basically know what's ahead or we wouldn't be in charge. If we're going to study the future, let's get the most preferable scenario on the table and then talk about what information might be out there that proves us right.

We have three major flavors of scenarios we usually identify:
- MERELY AWESOME (10% growth)
- SEXY AWESOME (20% growth)
- SAVING THE WORLD WITH OUR SEXY AWESOMENESS (70% GROWTH!!!)

Data collection is essential. When we have completed our X-ecutive Visioneering™ process, you will know which future is the most ideal for your purposes. And once we have created viral videos with cutting-edge graphics to illuminate for others what the future will look like, now it's time to engage our crack team of 23 year old unpaid analyst interns to fetch the appropriate data to back us up. They will find a variety of key indicators going in the upward direction, and these will serve as footnotes in our very physics journal-looking final report.

Make sure you provide the analysts ample recycling bins to serve as storage for the reams of data that don't show growth. That information was probably compiled by somebody in the midst of a major depression, besides.

>>>>>>>

The future intelligence view: Let the data drive the decision or don't bother

The entire point of going through one of these exercises is to be open to the outcome. If you automatically had any idea of what the future might actually require, it would be quite redundant to study any of this, no?

This is one of the most common distortions of this kind of analysis. Oh my...oh so common. In fact, excuse me while I wipe the blood from my forehead after banging my head into my desk contemplating the sheer number of times I have experienced this particular intellectual foible.

There is a constant caterwaul from futurists and competitive analysts alike - all analysts, really - that we are not taken seriously. I find often, it is more dire a situation than that. As opposed to the ideals of the Enlightenment we inherited from people who bled and died in their zeal, we are continuing the Medieval tradition of declaring reality to be a certain way, then expecting our men of science to bend all of their experiments accordingly. And while we have largely ceased the application of hot pokers, racks and horse drawings to those who don't appreciate our epistemic closure, ask yourself - what happened to those nice men who thought the Iraq War appeared to be a bad idea? What were the career paths of those in industry and government who actually saw the financial crisis cresting? If you were shorting credit default swaps from the vantage point of your own hedge fund, then you are reading this on your $50 million estate in the south of France. But if you were trying to ply that view from within a bureaucracy, chances are you were ejected from the bureaucratic organism like a putrescent clot of bacteria. The Future had been decided on, and either you were collecting data to support it, or your desk was moved to the middle of the parking deck.

Yes, I have actually heard tales of analysts' desks being moved to uncomfortable locales as a result of their delivering reports with uncomfortable findings. Oh, and then there's the trick of some extremely senior executive sitting down on the desk of a 25-year old analyst to ask if *maybe, just maybe they might have written that report incorrectly and would like to rethink and rewrite their conclusions. Not that it will hurt your career if you refuse, necessarily, it would just be very, very silly for you to arrive at a certain conclusion given the obviousness of what the data really means. Get the message? I'm glad we had this little talk you and I.*[49]

Real analysis rules. When analysts are just props in some public relations campaign to give credibility to unexamined decisions, we are getting that much closer to returning to our Medieval roots. It sounds dorky to be pro-analyst, but that's what I am. The stakes are very high indeed.

POSITIVE VALUES FOR THE FUTURE:

Critical thinking - Nobody trains people on how to be real analysts. How do you ask for real analysis or provide it when you have never even been given a set of guidelines or standards? It is high time that a professional methodology for research and analysis becomes part of every curriculum at schools that claim to train people for leadership positions. For anything resembling a successful future, we need people with the ability to think critically. Let us back that need up with education. Universities, companies, and government agencies all must be in on the act.

---

[49] *Think "Mesopotamia." Also popular when it comes to financial reporting.*

Tip 19

KEEP THE FINDINGS OF THE STUDY SECRET - DON'T TRY TO MAKE THE FINDINGS AVAILABLE THROUGHOUT THE ORGANIZATION

The future is not for the little people. The monkeys shouldn't be running the zoo when it comes to your predictological information. All strategical implication data should be kept within an elite group who will use it to shape policy in a way that is so subtle, neither your competitors nor your employees should know what you are up to. This way: maximum strategic tactical surprise ensues!

Look, you don't want your strategically secret information just hanging around waiting to be stolen, do you? No, once our galaxy-shattering insights have been distilled through futuristic visionation, these ideas should be safely carried through your organization in complete secrecy like you are trying to sneak a suitcase full of weapons-grade plutonium through Islamabad. You do NOT want this information to be subjected to the prying eyes of those who might actually think and act differently.

>>>>>>>

The future intelligence view: If foresight is to transform an organization, it needs to be on everyone's mind.

After fifteen years in the intelligence world, I understand discretion. I personally have signed a couple rain forests worth of nondisclosure agreements. So when I'm saying that we should re-examine policies of needless siloing of strategic information, I do not mean that you should post your next two years of strategic plans and a list of secret R&D projects on your Facebook fan page. I merely want to point out that far too few studies of the future see the light of day or are used as guides in an organization's operations. They start as elite activities, fine - but then they remain as information only used by the top few individuals. It should be no wonder, then, when we have organizations that are totally unaccustomed to thinking about the future.

This was brought home to me one day when working with the head of strategic planning for a major industrial manufacturer, one with operations in multiple countries and tens of thousands of employees. This executive told me that, out of a company that had an order of magnitude of more people than my hometown, only three people actually knew what the strategy of the company was.

I thought, "OK...wow, there must be a real brain trust going on there... wait, THREE? Only three people actually understand what you are doing in the marketplace? You have a bajillion in market cap, your stock is carried around the world, and the secret strategy is only understood by three people?" How is that a strategy? How does anybody ever act on that strategy if you are sworn to secrecy in a strategy love triangle?

I think I understand Google's strategy: dominate search, revolutionize advertising and offer free information services, which allows them to leverage search and advertising. I think I understand Apple's strategy: constantly innovate goods and services in the productivity and entertainment space with excellent customer experiences and new business models. Maybe Google is really angling to get in the mining business one day, and Apple's secret strategy is to commercialize patents from alien civilizations culminating in their perfection of healthcare that will allow humans to achieve immortality and perfect enlightenment. Perhaps only SIX PEOPLE hold this precious, precious knowledge. But I am willing to bet it is more that they are capitalizing on the advertising and the productivity/

entertainment businesses, respectively.

Some things are secret and require discretion. Precise dates for product launches, for example, can be a big deal for pharmaceutical product marketing, for new Apple releases, even for Hollywood blockbusters. There is even quite a science to enhancing your own launches and blunting competitive launches. This is, no doubt, why companies like Merck and Apple have well-recognized programs which test their information security to make sure nobody is leaking information. Note, however, that these issues requiring precision execution and total discretion are *tactical* in nature. They aren't really about the future, but about the down-and-dirty salesman-versus-salesman reality of ringing the cash register TODAY so we can all eat.

Trust me, your future is most likely transformative. Given the massive forces currently at play, how could it not be? The most important part of foresight is to change a culture to being more accepting of this kind of information.

An example of where future insight gets lost on the organization is in a managerial phenomenon known as *"credenzaware."* This phenomenon occurs when a 700-page work of exceeding brilliance is produced, illuminating the secrets of the universe, proving the link between the Knights Templar, Jack the Ripper, the Yakuza, Oprah Winfrey and the emergence of the iPad, resulting in the keys to winning every lottery and curing cancer 100% percent of the time, while also unlocking the secrets to writing hit pop songs- and then that work is placed in a binding, on a shelf, in a room, and then that room is burned down and the whole thing is never mentioned again.

This can happen one of two ways. Commonly, a giant project on the future is ordered, one that requires real insight and months of research and analysis. Sometime just before the conclusion of the project, some emergency pops up, either real or imagined, and when the work is delivered, everybody associated with getting insight into the organization is busy putting out fires. By the time things return to "normal" some weeks or months later, the folks who ordered the study may not even quite remember why they were curious about the future in the first place. Given the number of managerial emergencies that pop up, you can imagine the relative frequency of such a phenomenon.

Another round of credenzaware occurs following a merger. If you are at all familiar with history, you will recognize the all-too-regular technique of a conquering force defeating a nation and then burning the library so that their new subjects cannot even remember what it was like before the new boss arrived. Egypt, Maya, Laos, there are way too many sad stories of human progress lost to those who disdain any information which came from the old regime. While acquiring companies do not necessarily line up the employees of the junior company on crucifixes in the parking lot of the old headquarters,[50] "burning the library" is really quite popular. I remember producing a major report on the future of a certain type of retail and literally two days before the conclusion of the project, the client was acquired by a foreign rival. By sheer chance, our client contact was the ONLY survivor out of thousands who retained his employment in the new company. When we delivered our report to the new office, he thanked us profusely and let us down gently that we were probably the only people on earth who would read it, despite the fact that it pertained directly to the future operations of his new employer. You see, it was tainted with the weak stench of the vanquished enemy, assumed to be written in an indecipherable barbarian dialect, and considered useless by the new overlords.

In less nefarious sounding environments, the main problem is that documents about the future are produced, used for some dandy intellectual entertainment for a brief period of time, and then never used as a way to guide day-to-day thoughts or decision making. How can people create a better, more profitable future if they don't have the necessary intelligence to help create it?

Even in this world of ever-increasing transparency, nobody expects organizations to dump their most important secrets out in the open. Your available cash flow, your secret plans for the most advanced toaster the world has ever seen, nuclear launch codes - sure, keep that under wraps. Substantive discussions about the future need to be socialized in order to have maximum effect.

---

[50] *Well, layoffs aside*

POSITIVE VALUES FOR THE FUTURE:

Building a future-focused culture - It all comes back to culture. Futures is a total waste of time if your organizational culture will not allow this data to be used. And culture is only achieved through exposure, use, acceptance. It is pervasive and involves, ideally, the entire company. I think of 3M and Google, who create pervasive cultures of inventiveness, actually paying people to come up with their own ideas so they can create the future instead of watching it happen. I think about the Japanese auto manufacturers who created a culture of quality by paying bonuses to employees every time they found a way to improve inefficiencies and mistakes in manufacturing. Data about the future must be ubiquitous throughout a company and considered by all to be a great topic of discussion.

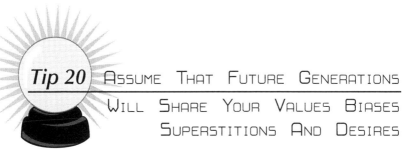

Tip 20 ASSUME THAT FUTURE GENERATIONS
WILL SHARE YOUR VALUES BIASES
SUPERSTITIONS AND DESIRES

Make sure that your future scenarios involve people who think exactly like you, sharing your values, economic assumptions, and technological preferences. After all, your experiences forged during the economic golden age in one of the top ten richest countries on earth will likely be applicable to all people, everywhere, for the next fifty years. Whether in the favelas of São Paolo, the call centers of Bangalore, the gilt halls of a Russian oligarch's London bungalow, or in the dimming post-industrial light of Buffalo, NY, people everywhere will believe globalization leads to bright futures, that technology will deliver us, and that modernity will always be better than tradition.

When seeing such people in 2030, 2050, 2100, make sure you picture people who think and act just like you. After all, you are all the pinnacle of human experience, so it only makes sense that future generations will pay no mind to the massive trends set to affect them in the coming decades.

>>>>>>>

The future intelligence view: The people in your future scenarios likely will not think like you.

There is a deep-seated fear about realizing that future generations will not share your assumptions. To truly accept that point is to become psychologically comfortable with mortality. This great train will keep going, though one day, we will not. Future generations are young today, being born today, will be born tomorrow, will be born long after we are gone. They will have their experiences, uncontaminated by the narratives we have told ourselves to make sense of it all. They will find love and create families according to the social structures of their day. Their job prospects will be shaped by tomorrow's economy, with its own strengths and weaknesses. Their assumptions of technology will be based on the number of problems they see it solve. Their success and failure will be shaped certainly by the world we leave, but also by their own autonomy. They will have their own narratives, and we will be but a fleeting memory in it.

There is a group of people from the future who will care about how we thought and felt in this moment - *historians*. That is the name we give to the people who search among the evidence left by the long-forgotten and attempt to analyze the world from their point of view. The reason we need historians is that when we look at past generations, they make no sense to us, really. Their assumptions are bewildering, their cognitive limitations perplexing, and their actions difficult to decipher. So we gather as much from them as possible to attempt to see the world from their bizarre perspective. Consider why, as people in the early 21st century, we might find our forebears' assumptions supremely unusual. For a person in 1750:

- You were likely the subject of a king who owed you very, very little consideration unless you were nobility. Otherwise you were the subject of a despot who owed you nothing at all. Things had *always* been this way.
- Wealth was enjoyed not because of merit, but because your parents had always had money.
- If you were a woman, you had a high likelihood of dying in childbirth.[51]
- Other fun for non-noble women - if your husband pre-deceased you,

126

a life of poverty was a near certainty.

- Your teeth would hurt most of your life; you would pull most of them before you were dead.
- Burying babies and young children was not a remarkable tragedy, but a regular sadness to endure.
- Travel beyond your tiny village was impossible unless you were rich or on a religious pilgrimage financed by the church.
- Education was fantastically expensive and rare.
- If you get pretty much any form of infection, you're dead. (OK, or we could just hack off a significant part of your body. And you'll die later. Enjoy the peg-leg!)
- Have you been interested in being burned, tortured, jailed, or otherwise outcast from society? Disagree with the church in public.

The list, obviously, could go on. *Why would these people have the same assumptions as people born in 1990?* Which assumptions would these people living just before the dawn of the Enlightenment share with people who grew up with high-speed internet, cheap air travel, targeted drugs with minimal side effects, with most of their teeth in their head, with all of their siblings still alive, with both parents still alive, with a life expectancy of 87 years?

In other words: imagine how different Generation Y is from your generation. Now imagine, the people in your future scenarios will be weirder than that.

POSITIVE VALUES FOR THE FUTURE:

Detachment - To put ourselves in the mindset to freely consider the future, we cannot really be players in the game. Our egos cannot come for the trip, even if the future concerns us greatly. Detachment allows us the freedom to consider positive and negative futures without immediately having a reaction. We can imagine other people on their journeys without judgment. Then, we can return to the present day and make decisions that *do* involve us - though the analysis will be much improved.

---

[51] *Many women in the West would go into labor in their finest gowns, their beds covered in the best lace in the house so that if they died, they would leave a nice scene. THAT IS WAY DEPRESSING. HOORAY OBSTETRICS, MICROBIOLOGY AND MODERN PHARMACEUTICALS.*

Tip 21 CONFUSE SEXY WITH IMPORTANT

G aze into the face of the sexy future: it's glassy, glossy, and digital. It is a gadget available to 0.1% of consumers around the world. The future will be defined by the next generation of these gadgets.

Make sure that your laser-focus on sexy is unbroken by any moribund topics such as fertilizer or rice or coal or railroads or industrial manufacturing or sea shipping. Remember, we're in a post-industrial future, and so industrial things should best be left to unthinking drones, preferably in a country with lax environmental regulation. Until Fast Company and WIRED start making a big deal out of turnips and ball-bearings, you should be concerned mainly with 8G-capable finger top e-readers.

The sexy future is a great source of scenario building since, after all, the graphic design you can do in support of your visions can just drip with next-generation cool. Since we know that the future will be driven by elite consumer trends rather than boring stuff like fish stocks and natural gas infrastructure, make sure that your scenarios feature the right images. The ideal images should portray a world that is a cross between a 1980s David Bowie music video and a *Martha Stewart Living* catalog.

As a corollary to this, please, please do not feature rural people, working class people, or people from uncool countries. The sexy future is generally only happening in cities where a one-bedroom apartment costs around 3000 euros a month - think London, Tokyo, Paris, West Hollywood, Hong Kong. Include Dubai if it doesn't sink into the sea or get swallowed by the desert. Definitely don't get any more redneck than Singapore.

An exception to this rule - your future visions may feature rural farmers squatted around a malfunctioning well looking for decreasingly available water, but only if you show them using a shiny knuckletop tablet computer with a look of wonder on their faces. If their future isn't sexy for some reason, then surely they will be sitting around wishing that it was. It's like Oscar Wilde said, "Take care of the luxuries, and the water shortages and $270 barrels of oil will take care of themselves."

>>>>>>>

The future intelligence view: The future is more down-and-dirty than sexy.

The media seems to only report on matters of the future if they are cool or handsome.

I blame my generation, the Internet and video games.

There is so much mind-blowing stuff going on every day 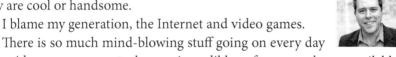 with video games, smart phones, incredible software packages available online and around the world, that you could be forgiven for getting distracted by the sheer cool factor. Consider the point of view of my people, Generation X. After watching Star Wars for the fifty-eighth time, we survived and thrived because of Pong and Atari and AM/FM radios, and *now* you walk into the electronics store and see 62 inch 3D televisions and Xbox 720s and Blue-Ray and iPhones with HD video and...well, you'll forgive us if we get so excited that all we want to do is talk about how awesome the new 3D massively-multiplayer Star Wars game is, which we will broadcast on video using our new phones. If you had shown us this when we were six years old, we would have lost our minds. So today, we are easily distracted by this kind of thing.

This is, of course, no excuse for the fact that most people have lost all sight of the industrial system which underpins our society. There is very little ability among most people to prioritize which goods actually allow us to function. Sexy looking consumer electronics suck up a significant percentage of the oxygen in media coverage of business. Many, though, fail to perceive that you could throw all of your plasma/LCD/nanomatrix teevees in the river and change pretty much nothing about the world. The world will not tremble from having to step back to 480 pixel television resolution for a month. Try, however, to spend a day without industrial lubricant. Make an attempt to live without goods that arrive via container ships. Cut your country off from coal for a couple weeks. See what happens.

When we provide futuring exercises for leaders, our first step is always to diagram all of the activities that go into their business - in pointillistic detail. Once you dive in beyond the surface, you always end up at the awesome complexity of down and dirty industrial economics. The world, at the end of the day, is still about extracting resources from the Earth's crust, processing them, refining them through manufacturing and delivering them around the world. Thus, the vast majority of the world's activity concerns such non-sexy topics as: copper, bauxite, iron, wood, coal, natural gas, oil, rail, trucking, farming, warehousing, logistics, and so forth. Changes in the vital infrastructure of your business may, in fact, be an even greater long-term driver of competition than product innovation.

One of my greatest personal successes as a futurist was actually turning a company's attention away from the flashy future of shiny tech to the dirty reality of 19th century limitations. You see, the client made consumer goods for which a high-level of technical innovation is expected. Looking at the long-term future of their competition, they expected to trawl weak signals for signs of competitors launching new products with their patents in Xtreme Nanotech Awesomeness.[52] When we tore apart the various factors which underpinned the whole enterprise, innovations included, the executives became increasingly aware that maybe their factories were located in places where water would soon become scarce and more expensive. But then, so were their competitors. Ultimately, they figured that

---

[52] *Xtreme Nanotech Awesomeness is what will lead to the Singularity, you know.*

they needed to hedge their bets on shiny, attention grabbing new geegaws with smart investments in new, ecologically-sound factories in *other places*.

This is the kind of insight that does not bear fruit right away. The dirty, uncool stuff is usually about infrastructure, and infrastructure is usually pretty pricey. It takes years to build, a decade or more to amortize, and creates the competitive advantage that can last a generation. It is not easy, since it doesn't just involve throwing some new tools into a Chinese factory to make the next product release *even more awesomer*. But one of these days, one of those companies is going to be rather successful and the other could very well be buying expensive water or building factories at the last minute.

Another reason the future is about coal rather than gadgets. The Chinese, Indian and U.S. economies will be running on the sooty black stuff, not to mention other countries seeking electrical power. We have hundreds of years worth of coal without even looking hard, and no other source is as reliable or available to meet the scale of energy demands to come.

Before the green party members have a stroke, I am not saying I think this is a particularly great thing, for reasons of pollution and climate change, just that the dominance of coal is highly likely. But you see, *that is not a very cool thing to say about the future.*

A cool, sexy thing to say about the future would be, *"Did you know that chemists in the Netherlands are looking for ways to turn hypocrisy and procrastination into pure, carbon-neutral fuel for cars! It could be the energy of the future!"* You could increase your hipness quotient by talking about "growing our energy" in the form of corn-, sugar-cane- or switchgrass-based biofuels. You see, biofuel has "bio" in it, which is very green, and quite cool too. Make sure to skip the fact that more energy in the form of fertilizer and farm machinery would go into its production than would ever come out, because then people would feel even more depressed. Undeterred, you might then talk about the prospect of nanotechnology giving us some material that could cover our highways with a material that is simultaneously tough and ALSO solar panels which are by definition connected to our towns and cities!!! These things are forward-thinking, futuristic, hip, cool.

Reality isn't cool, it's just reality. The reality of energy is that there is no single forecast of merit about the future supply and demand of energy that suggests that renewables will make up a significant percentage of the market in the future. It breaks down by the chart below, courtesy of the EIA.

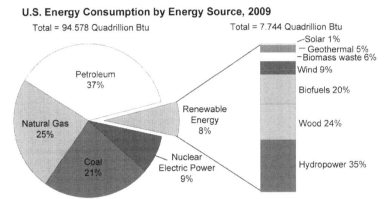

U.S. Energy Consumption by Energy Source, 2009

Total = 94.578 Quadrillion Btu   Total = 7.744 Quadrillion Btu

Petroleum 37%

Natural Gas 25%

Coal 21%

Renewable Energy 8%

Nuclear Electric Power 9%

Solar 1%
Geothermal 5%
Biomass waste 6%
Wind 9%
Biofuels 20%
Wood 24%
Hydropower 35%

Note: Sum of components may not equal 100% due to independent rounding.
Source: U.S. Energy Information Administration, *Annual Energy Review 2009*, Table 1.3, Primary Energy Consumption by Energy Source, 1949-2009 (August 2010).

So, that is a whole lotta coal, a whole bunch of oil for the worldwide vehicle fleet, natural gas for electrical generation and home heating, a bit of nuclear for energy, and the remainder - 13% - is renewables, the majority of which is combustible biomass.

By 2035, most of the agencies and groups which forecast energy markets predict that the mix of energy sources will be...*just about the same.* Whatever technological innovations lay in wait for solar and wind, they occupy such a small percentage of the supply, that it is extremely improbable that they will change industry in the coming decades. This means that countries need to anticipate petroleum shortages and the environmental effects of coal - at the very least. The chances of a magic, sexy technology bailing us out of our global predicament is exceedingly unlikely.

That is important. It is not sexy. There is no equivalent of the Consumer Electronics Show for energy or sewage. Even when scientists come up with something really quite innovative like the guys who learned to make sweet crude oil out of turkey guts,[53] it doesn't receive nearly the excitement of Frogger being suddenly available on our phones. Not sexy enough. But it

---

[53] *I am not making this up! Do a Google search.*

sure ought to be important enough.

If you are a leader, you should be able to distinguish between these two concepts.

POSITIVE VALUES FOR THE FUTURE:

Maturity - Coal? Sewage? Ball bearings? Absolutely none of that sounds any fun. And too bad. Future-focused leaders can understand the priorities of a complex, ever-changing world. The media that covers such issues, should they want to take part in creating a society that is robust and intelligent, might also produce content for mature adults who are actively taking part in making this world go 'round. As it stands, most people are presented with a constant stream of entertainment, whether it is reality television or the cable business news that treats the day's stock prices like a spectator sport on the level of Ultimate Fighting. The unfortunate principle underlying this stream of information is that people are uninterested in that which really allows their communities to function. We are told, implicitly, that it is for someone else more responsible...somewhere...to handle. If we are to lead our civilization into the future, we must spread the responsibility around. We need to treat people like mature adults and they need to act like them.

Roots - Those who would make decisions for our collective future must understand the world from the ground up. That includes, by definition, a comprehension of just how down and dirty the whole operation really is: soil, sewage, raw materials, brute logistics. You may have no idea just how rare such an appreciation is in the world of intellectuals. I worked at a think tank where I was the only person in the room ever to have done manual labor of any sort. I was the only person who could roughly describe how food arrived at grocery stores. I was the only person who had ever come home dirty because of his job. It was no surprise, then, when I heard people who possessed great fluency in describing the brave new world of social-mediafied internetweb self-branding, but expressed no love for describing the role of fertilizer in this same brave new world. Let's get it straight: the world works just fine without social media, and not at all without farming. Get back to your roots if you want to know the future.

NEVER SUGGEST THE WHOLE
MODEL MAY BE CHANGING

I n his wonderfully predictive book *The End of History and the Last Man,* Francis Fukuyama told us we were at the end of history and that we awesomely capitalistic non-communists won while everybody else lost.. He's right, we did win, we ran the victory lap, and now there should be no major strategic shifts to come. Also, I know him from the lecture circuit, he's a charming, wonderful guy, and I'll be the last to challenge him in public.

This is why when you are looking out in the future, the worst thing you can do is suggest that the entire dynamic of the world is shifting. Pick one or two elements and describe their incremental changes, but don't hyperventilate about the system no longer working the same way. The system works the way it does because it was designed by wise, omniscient people in the past, and you shouldn't get into the habit of challenging their superiority just because you want to imagine a different future for the world.

That said, there are a few shifts you can feel at liberty to describe:

Exception Number One: The New Era of Awesome Technology! Feel free to discuss how some glossy device will change the world while leaving the vast majority of its industrial and economic realities in tact! Lavish florid and inventive prose on the new gadget, relishing with abandon how it will be more fun and make existing processes more efficient. Extra points if you suggest that the device could result in world peace or ubiquitous, free, high-quality education.

Exception Number Two: The New Era of X-Treme Competition! It is always the right time to tell audiences that we're entering the most competitive world in history. In this Tolkienesque realm of clashing forces, you will be expected to cut costs while doing less with more. Adding to the hero's journey, consumers will be more demanding than ever, while competition that looks and acts just like our company swarms us like gaggles of wild dragons. You get extra points if you tell your audience of ambitious workaholics that in the future they will really, really need to buckle down over and above their current 92 hour work weeks.

Exception Number Three: The New Era of the Choosy Consumer! You may always tell people about the unprecedented universe of ultra-demanding consumers. They don't just want mocha soy half-twist biofuel coffee drinks - you heard me - they want a mocha soy-rice switchgrass Kenya AA latte that is actually matched to their genotype through a genetic profile they have assigned to their customer loyalty card. In this crazy galaxy with its own laws of physics, people are defined by their clothing choices, their self-esteem is tied up in their hubcap preference, and their smartphone case had better match their eyes. Sure, they may be following a type of lifestyle that has been essentially unchanged since the postwar consumerist 1950s, but they are now ultra-choosy and you need to be able to respond on a nanosecond's notice to their needs.

Other than those shifts, I think your assumptions should remain unmolested for decades to come.
>>>>>>>

The future intellgence view: **In a world of transformation you will likely need to change something pretty major.**

I find that discussions about the future hinge on whether we are looking at incremental shifts or transformative changes. The vast majority of information we receive through the media is geared toward incrementalism. This only makes sense given the historical tendency toward change versus stasis. Almost everybody currently working the levers of our industrial society has grown up in a period of constant expansion of the same paradigm. The United States, with its explosive Post-War growth, the prosperous decades of "les trente glorieuses" in France, the re-emergence of Germany and Japan - even China, India and Latin America - have basically joined the same paradigm that brought the Industrial West to stability and prosperity.

The thing is, this is not normal. History is more defined by all the radical changes that tend to sweep our social and economic systems. A sixty-year period of relative success and stability is freakish. In the Industrial West, most people in positions of power have never had to experience managing the normal world of whiplash change that has been more the rule than the exception. That said, the phrase "THIS CHANGES EVERYTHING" is used glibly in our society for everything from new video game consoles to voice activated car locks. The thing is, there have been times in history when the entire paradigm actually *has* been changed. Consider the launch of the last video game format with:

- The rise and fall of the Roman Empire
- Schism of the Christian church
- The age of exploration
- The scientific revolution
- The nuclear age
- Industrialism
- The information age

Yes, tablet computers are neat and portable, but frankly the scientific method had a bit more of a pervasive effect on humanity when it comes to "changing everything."

We humans are smart in general. People who end up as leaders in bureaucracies often exhibit a certain *type* of intelligence. Math, communications, organization - even a taste for complexity and a hint of appreciation for ambiguity. Being "smart" in such a framework is a full-time job. So full-time, in fact, that it may make it difficult to see the framework change. The fundamental alteration of the paradigm means that what makes you smart and effective today might not matter too much in the next framework.

One of the chief values of futurism is to show you how entire systems might change, especially where new winners and losers might be concerned. These conversations are deep and philosophical, but do not be mistaken, there are very practical implications for future competition contained in such musings. So let's get PRACTICAL: what happens when a business must change its model in a transformative way?

First, we should get some terms straight. A business model is not just about what kinds of products you are bringing to market. It is not about targeting different customers with the same products. A new business model occurs when your position in the value chain changes radically and you ask for money in new ways, for different reasons, from different customers. When the world is changing in a transformative way, you really do have two choices: evolve along with it, or keep doing what you are doing. Both are valid, though both seem to have different outcomes.

A little mom-and-pop company called International Business Machines may be one of the positive examples of true business model transformation. They took a company from a producer of hardware to a provider of solutions in a period of a few years. Imagine the mindset that Louis Gerstner managed to change and the tactical management required to make it stick. IBM cut billions in expenses and raised cash by selling assets, returning the company to solvency. He stopped a plan to break up the company into several operating units and refocused its strategy on services and software. Today, the company is making money on its intellectual assets, the unrivaled understanding of how IT acts as infrastructure to economic activity, often using hardware from other companies, if it makes sense. The total story fits inside a single paragraph, but imagine the shock to an organization this would cause. There is a reason it is still a famous business case.

I would like to take this moment to thank the music industry for continuing to serve as a perfect example of the penalties for not seeing the transformative change of its business model in advance. I've been milking this one for a decade, and they still entertain me by continuing to sue people, continuing to lose 15% a year in revenue, and continuing to go down with the ship. The MP3 changed their position in the value chain forever, and they opted to do essentially nothing. They are now joined by bookstores and publishers in their ultimate fate.

Dare to talk about the real, knotty, nasty, complex changes that are on the horizon. Your shareholders will thank you one day.

POSITIVE VALUES FOR THE FUTURE:

Holism - In our ultra-specialized world, we are economically motivated to sacrifice a holistic view of the world in order to concentrate on a niche that will provide us with an income. This goes for companies as well as individual people. This is only natural, but it tempts us away from seeing things as a complex ecosystem, which is the only way to have any predictive capability about the future these days. That temptation will come in the form of focusing on an incremental future, one that only involves slightly cooler phones, personalized steering wheel covers, and other inconsequential microtrends. If we are to understand the future and define our role in it, we must regain the ability to think in terms of whole systems. We must be able to describe macroshifts with ample time to react. The conversations are more interesting than the microtrends about hot colors and buzzwords, anyway; you could have even more fun this way.

Tip 23

COMMUNICATE THE FUTURE
IN THE MOST ABSTRACT,
JARGONY, IGNORABLE LANGUAGE

I f the future is described in a way that makes sense to the average person, chances are you aren't that clever. Unless you're a fan of making minimum wage, I'd be bumping up the clever quotient in your forecasting. The use of impenetrable jargon is a wonderful way to increase the façade of cleverness you will require to be taken seriously as a guru of predictological futureness.

You have a couple types of jargon from which to choose:

TODAY'S JARGON
- Derivatives
- 8G
- Twitcasting
- Enhanced interrogation
- Quantitative easing
- Growth

TOMORROW'S JARGON
- Marketcasting

- Viralifing
- In a flatness place
- Blarging
- 4D-10G-90QHz

To improve your forecast writing, mix and match these terms to achieve futurey greatness:

- *The smart hedge funds are exploiting economies currently in a flatness place to expand the weak signals of their exposure in derivatives. Innovation strategy mindshare growth.*
- *If the companies of tomorrow want to use marketcasting in its most profitable way, to make sure they are viralifying their brands, there is no way they can ignore 4D and 10G communications and their powerful applications for use in blarging. Innovation strategy mindshare growth.*

Another excellent option for communication is the use of overly complex language so pretentious that it would make a PhD candidate in comparative transgender literature retch. A special guideline here is to never say anything definite about what is happening, only make commentary about the world from a meta-analytical distance of seven light-years.

- *While many people attempt to obtain analytical scope from a wikimacroeconomics perspective, it should be evident that the very nature of volition is in constant evolution. The world's populations, all at once united and very distinct in their various approaches to effort production are aligned as far as connectedness. More than ever, it is clear that all activity in the dynamic of money alignment will be COORDINATED by collaboration, changing the very manner in which we think of profit. This has been on the minds of well-thinking CEOs for years now, and it would be unwise for others not to cogitate on what is no doubt our shared future. Innovation strategy mindshare growth.*

The client's check will have cleared before they have even understood the earth-shattering complexities of these predictological insights, further demonstrating your courageous, strategicky brilliance.

Obviously, make sure they have not post-dated the check.

>>>>>>>

The future intelligence view: Tell it to them straight.

Please read the following statements about the future to any person living in your neighborhood, irrespective of age or level of education.

- We're running out of water on most continents, which we really need.
- Every bit piece of writing, music and film ever created will be available digitally, everywhere on earth, sometime this century.
- The Baby Boom generation is huge, and getting old quick, and the cost of their healthcare will bankrupt most countries.

Nobody needs to consult a thesaurus to understand what I have just written. Nor do they need to call their niece in Silicon Valley or neighbor's kid in Williamsburg, Brooklyn to receive a primer in the slang of the last five minutes. And yet, these are powerful, relevant, and all about the future.

It is tempting to write about the future in terms of mushy language and the faddish terminology of the minute. Telling people the future straight can be jarring for both parties, and florid language helps cushion the blow. It depends on your audience and what you want them to know. If you want to look cool, jargon is the way to go. If you want to discuss the future, tell it to people straight. Make your conclusions awesomely simple, and save the verbosity for the discussion of what it means, since that topic is by nature less defined.

My mentor Joseph Coates taught me an interesting writing technique, specifically for discussing the future, but also a good idea for any writing in the English language.

Whenever possible, use Anglo-Saxon words versus their Greco-Roman counterparts.

Now, unless you are a linguist accustomed to tearing apart the etymology of words, this may actually take a bit of thinking.

Acquire -> GET

Possess -> HAVE

Reduce -> LOSE

Challenges -> BIG PROBLEMS

Consider it, which would you rather get, a "warm welcome" or a "cordial salutation?" They mean the same thing in the abstract - but not to native speakers of English. In almost every situation, the Greco-Roman words that make up half of the language are used to show superiority of education and to create a layer of distance.

Think of any interaction with a bureaucrat. Let's say the unemployment office. If you have exceeded the limit of your time on the dole[54] they will not say, *"Hey, you've been out of a job for too long, so we're not giving you any more money."* Instead they explain, *"Pursuant to your exceeding the time limits accorded to our program, your benefits are hereby terminated."* It's the same message, *Jack - get yourself a job, because we ain't sending checks no more.* In reality, the message is neither more polite nor easier to take just because the words used are multisyllabic. However, the benefit here is in providing a layer of comfort to the bureaucrat delivering the message - at once he/she can distance him/herself from the transaction while also claiming the high ground of superiority through a more sophisticated choice of words.

I have a very likely explanation for this dynamic based entirely on my amateur status as a historian and linguist.[55] The Romans have forever been in contact and conflict with the Germanic tribes to the north. Ultimately, it is those Germanic tribes who dominate the majority of Roman imperial territory in Gaul and Brittania. Their languages developed by merging tribal words with loan words for concepts not existing in their vocabularies, like almost all languages. No doubt in the centuries of contact, the Germanic tribes developed the habit of using their own words for familiar things and Roman words for more complex concepts that pertained to the

---

[54] *Pour les lecteurs français: Aux États-Unis il n'est possible de toucher à la securité sociale à vie. Nous regrettons le choc.*

[55] *Not to be trusted.*

management of a global empire, especially politics and accounting. As the English language developed into its own unique amalgam of German and Romance roots, it seems likely that people also inherited the prejudices of their forebears, using warm and familiar Anglo-Saxon terms for friends and Greco-Roman words for people they want to keep at bay, such as foreign invaders. So even today, we prefer the short, powerful words of the tribes over the sterile language of diplomats and lawyers.

So that's what I'm saying, people. No nonsense, just call it like you see it if you want your story of the future to have a lot of punch.

POSITIVE VALUES FOR THE FUTURE:

Clarity - With 24/7 media, there is already enough talking. Be clear, be fearless, and be unequivocal.

Courage - The above sentiment should be pretty frightening to you. There is a very good reason we couch some statements in softening language: POLITICS. If you have been working longer than five minutes, you know that your results vary wildly depending on who you talk to and how you put things. It is just that such niceties may not always carry the urgency required in our rapidly evolving world. To know the difference of when to be nice and when to be direct will take real guts.

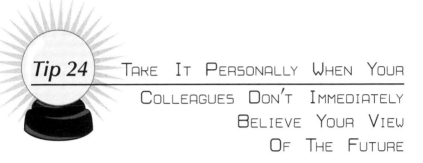

Tip 24 — Take It Personally When Your Colleagues Don't Immediately Believe Your View Of The Future

Sure, you're dumping the future on people, but that's no reason for them to need to process it. They should, by dint of your awesome charisma and credibility-assuring past successes, accept your view **immediately**.

Make sure that you treat all resistance to the future with the bureaucratic hostility it deserves. I mean, you've gone to all this trouble to outline a brilliant future and here your colleagues go asking for supporting evidence and criticizing the potential implications of your futuristic prognostimation. The nerve.

>>>>>>>

The future intelligence view: Make the case for change

Convincing gigantic bureaucracies to have a shift of mindset takes time, patience and maturity. Overall you need to understand, once again, the mindset of bureaucracy if you want to participate in the arduous task of helping it evolve.

I am inspired by the thinking of an American consultant who specializes in change management, Rick Maurer.[56] While the term "change management" has largely become a term of profanity in my mind given the number of frauds associated with the movement, Maurer's ideas are very helpful for getting people to accept ideas about the future. Most powerful of his concepts is "making the case for change," the notion that simply dumping new ideas or *fait accompli* changes in direction are totally futile if you do not take the psychology of change into account. People accept change over different time frames, sort of like the amount of time it took your various family members to buy mobile telephones.[57] You should plan on all acceptance of your foresight coming in waves as you present lots of data and analysis, build credibility, think broadly and involve stakeholders, and practice zen-like patience.

POSITIVE VALUES FOR THE FUTURE:

Appreciation for the complex psychology of human beings - We are unfathomably tricky creatures, no? And we are not even delving into the added difficulty of communicating change between cultures. That would be a whole 'nother book. Are you feeling a bit like you are preparing to be a therapist? It's OK, me too sometimes.

---

[56] *Check out http://www.beyondresistance.com*

[57] *Boy, this example will not age well if this book is still in print in ten years.*

Tip 25

Don't let this future stuff get out of hand. In our view, this should be an occasional activity - essential, certainly, but best used sparingly. Remember, it's about predicting the future YOU want, not about creating a constant, real-time, ever-evolving intelligence practice that is at the heart of your organizational operations. Once you get the appropriate vision of just how you're going to end up even sexier and more important by 2050, you can stop it with the future thing and get back to the quarterly performance metrics.

Just make sure it's me you call when you get back around to thinking about the future next time!

>>>>>>>

The future intelligence view: **Every organizational culture should be future-focused, every day.**

Making a future-focused organization is about changing the culture of how you and your colleagues think and talk with each other about uncertainty. It is not about applying arcane and difficult techniques.

You want techniques? Brother, sister, WE GOT TECHNIQUES. Go check out the Jerry Glenn compendium of every futurist technique ever invented, available on CD-ROM with any copy of "The State of the Future" report that gets rolled out to the United Nations.[58] As I proposed at the beginning of this book, these techniques: forecasting, backcasting, Delphi, impact-probability, all that - it is not that hard and it's all available information. You can grab your colleagues, hold them up at shotgun-point and force them to write a 23,000 page report on the future of your industry that will light the way for profit. But you probably won't. The majority of organizations do not have a culture that supports caring about this kind of information. And that is what needs changing.

This is about a mindset that extends beyond profitable management of a company; of the effective leadership of a non-profit; of stewardship of government resources. This is about the survival of a species. It can also be use d to work on the success of individuals in that species, but I submit that it is no longer optional, just suitable to dust off every decade or so.

Do you know what caused the discipline of futures to be born in the first place? Was it used to predict video game sales? Were people originally working on scenarios for the kitchen of the future? Developing contingency plans for public health?

Nope: Nukes. We invented nuclear weapons in the early 1940s and about ten years later it became terrifyingly clear to defense analysts that it would be impossible to contain the proliferation of these devices. This meant that geopolitics as we knew it had completely changed and our ways of thinking were outdated. We could no longer predict the future based on the past, and the consequence of ignorant action was now - everybody dies horribly, all at once.

Hence the development of scenarios, forecasts, backcasts, Delphi studies, technology assessment and all the rest of the techniques designed to get our thinking evolving as fast as the world of science and technology. A futurist by the name of Herman Kahn worked for the Rand Corporation, a think tank working for the U.S. Department of Defense. He was really the first intellectual willing to imagine horrible outcomes and talk about them

---

[58] *http://www.millennium-project.org/millennium/publications.html.*

with a dispassionate approach. He produced vivid scenarios of the various types of nuclear exchanges, potential triggers, even the famous concept of "nuclear winter" in which case nothing would grow and we would all starve to death even if we weren't incinerated or irradiated directly by nuclear blasts. He gave numbers of casualties, estimates of which continents would be unlivable and for how long. These possible futures were dire enough that people had to take the future seriously. It did not seem frivolous, optional, or beside the point.

Today's geopolitical and economic complexity promises opportunities and threats every bit as important as nuclear proliferation. We may have spent the last few decades in a period of relative stability, but you can point to several periods throughout history that were stable before devolving into strife. And with today's complexity, the process of destabilization will likely happen faster than ever before. We have been lulled into a sense of false security by our recent successes. Balance must be returned to how we think about what is next.

This is not to say that every organizational culture is supposed to be filled with a bunch of drunken melancholy poets, loaded on absinthe and lamenting the inevitable fate of man. There is plenty of money to be made, too. Our world is so full of inefficiencies in matters ranging from education to energy to agriculture, that those who step in to offer solutions in the face of systems that have been made obsolete will find fertile fields indeed. You see, organizations that shut out all information of negative futures usually also cannot handle forecasts of positive futures either. Stability, to these organizations, is not just denying the potential for strife, but also refusing to seize new opportunities for fear of upsetting the current order.

A future-focused culture is, at the end of the day, balanced. It is neither expecting to be saved by new technologies, as some did in the 20th century, nor does it become obsessed with gloom and doom, as some slip into today. Such a culture is knowledgeable about the past, realistic about the present, and brave in the face of the uncertainties of what is next. It is, in a word, *mature*. And so, this culture does not view the future as a fashionable interest in stable times, but a permanent philosophy.

This can only come from leaders. It can bubble up from the ranks of our bureaucracies, though experience tells us that it can only flourish when leaders make the mental transition themselves.

POSITIVE VALUES FOR THE FUTURE:

Commitment - The only way to build organizations that are robust and resilient is for leadership to exhibit a profound commitment to a future-focused culture. And this has nothing to do with whichever hierarchy you work for today - it is about individuals embracing this view and carrying it with them wherever they go in matters public and private.

CODA

What next? Will we forge forth to really predict the future and WIN?

I hope we come to see complexities and failures of the current moment as a watershed in how we perceive bureaucracies and their collective logic. It is time to understand why we have not yet created a near-ubiquity of future-oriented organizations, and also time to understand that it still remains possible to reach this height as we grow in maturity as a world culture.

You see, behind every satire is optimism biding its time. I believe that we can have a renaissance in management, one that takes into account the realities of human behavior more than convenient mythologies. To continue on our current path of shallow intellectual disciplines is to take an enormous risk given the daunting complexity we face. So to repeat the mantra of futurists past and present, we know we should look at the future, we know we have the tools - now it is time to go do it.

One thing is for sure: it is not about data. Though there are limitations, as we have pointed out, there is generally more data out there than could possibly be digested. In the words of my colleague Arik Johnson, chairman of Aurora WDC and a thoughtleader in the world of intelligence, we have surpassed the era of data scarcity. According to Johnson, competitive advantage went to the leader with an *asymmetry of information* - whoever had the best intelligence networks feeding the most information emerged victorious. We are now in the area of *asymmetry of analysis*, with the competitive advantage going to those who can interpret data to their advantage better than their rivals. I couldn't agree more.

We live in an era that cries out for real leaders, men and women who can master the daily skills of management while constantly handling new intelligence about a changing world and also balancing a historical perspective and empathy for all those connected to their enterprise. There is no question, this is a tall order.

But if you are going to dream of a future, why not dream of an ideal one? Here is what my ideal future looks like. We must collectively and individually:

- Create livable cities that are designed for maximum public health, commerce, energy efficiency, and civic participation.
- Design economies that live within local resource constraints, i.e. are sustainable.
- Provide basic healthcare to all citizens in a way that does not bankrupt our institutions, especially to the unprecedented number of people over the age of 65.
- Assure ample opportunities for young people to integrate into their societies after an appropriate education, no matter the social caste into which they were born.
- Build and measure an economy that is designed around real gains in standard of living for the billions excluded from the current system, instead of fake financialized book-cooking.
- Continue the assurance of human rights in every nation on earth, spreading the notion of universally-true, sacrosanct freedoms.
- Deepen our understanding of the sciences to provide insight to future generations.
- Return the arts to their rightful place as the greatest achievement of human kind.

There is more work to do, but those are quite enough goals for the moment.

I wish you all the best in creating your own ideal future.

ACKNOWLEDGEMENTS:

Dr. P. Hughes Egon would like to thank the following for years of moral support and fantastic dinner parties: Sean Combs, the Dalai Lama, Thomas Friedman, Tony Hayward, Antonin Scalia, Bill Clinton, the Blue Man Group, Jiang Zemin, Barbra Streisand, the Honorable Justin Bieber, Silvio Berlusconi, Katy Perry, "Chainsaw Al" Dunlop, Jean-Marie LePen, Gwyneth Paltrow, Malcolm Gladwell, and 50 Cent.

Eric Garland would like to thank:

Steve Woods and Chad Forbis at the Starbucks in Valley Park, Missouri (corner of Big Bend and Dougherty Ferry) for providing the venue in which to ghost write Dr. Egon's latest blockbuster. Thank you for not enforcing city ordinances against loitering.

For support both intellectual and emotional he would like to acknowledge Craig Arneson, Gregor Macdonald, Lynne Puetz, Chris Largent, Scott Anderson, Arik and Derek Johnson, Tim Wood Powell, Sazen Khuker, Marilyn Davis, Philippe Juré, Jaime Salazar, Josette Bruffaerts-Thomas, August Jackson, Sue Snyder, April Swain, Lee Robinson, Jon Michael Ryan. And all the rest of you, you're on notice.

Special thanks to my mother, Marilyn Garland. She got hosed in the acknowledgements section of my last book.

Extra special thanks to William Garland for providing the sleep deprivation which led to the psychic break that produced this work.

ABOUT THE GHOST WRITER

Eric Garland is a professional Latin jazz bassist who has worked in competitive intelligence and strategic forecasting for a couple of decades now. In between salsa gigs, he provides trend analysis for dozens of huge companies you have heard of, quite a few governments, two school boards, and one constitutional monarchy.

Eric plays regularly with Gato & the Palenke Music Company, Verny Varela, Los del Barrio, the DC Latin Jazz All-Stars, Sin Miedo, and is the author of *Future, Inc: How Businesses Can Anticipate and Profit from What's NEXT*. He has a Master's degree that was expensive which nobody ever asks about. He splits his time between St Louis, Washington DC, Paris, Montreal, Vermont, and wherever they have really great guitar stores.

Eric plays John Suhr guitars, Fender, Pedulla and Ampeg basses, as well as using Headstrong, Polytone, David Eden and Genz Benz amplifiers.

OTHER BOOKS BY ERIC GARLAND

Future Intelligence: How Business Can Anticipate and Profit from What's Next